The Amazing Adventures of
MR. GRANT MONEY

STRIVE press

Dear Reader,

Thank you for joining us on this exciting journey with The Amazing Adventures of Mr. Grant Money. I'm thrilled to share the valuable insights and transformative lessons within these pages—lessons that have empowered countless students, educators, and organizations to achieve remarkable success in securing scholarships and grant funding.

Scholarships and grants are powerful tools for opening doors to opportunity, and this book is designed to be your trusted companion as you navigate the intricate world of funding for education. Within these stories, you'll find not just engaging narratives but essential lessons and strategies to guide you and your students toward securing the financial support needed to achieve your academic goals.

This book is more than a collection of stories—it's part of a comprehensive approach to scholarship and grant education. As you read and engage with the exercises, I hope you discover actionable strategies and inspiration to elevate your efforts to new heights.

I'd also like to introduce you to an invaluable resource: our specially curated content on the Mr. Grant Money website. At www.mrgrantmoney.com/college-scholarships, you'll find in-depth information, book reviews, bonus content, and resources to help you go even further. This is just one book in a five-part series, each designed as part of a comprehensive curriculum that can guide you and your students through an entire year of training in grant and scholarship acquisition.

When you visit our website, be sure to check out the blog, where you'll find additional stories and articles. You'll also enjoy our deep-dive interviews and podcast-style discussions that make learning both enjoyable and engaging. For schools and organizations interested in maximizing the impact of this curriculum, I encourage you to explore our licensing program, which provides access to exclusive resources, saves time, and helps you make the most of these lessons.

Finally, because we believe learning should be both fun and memorable, don't miss the Mr. Grant Money music collection—a perfect complement to this educational journey. With its upbeat tracks and inspirational messages, the music is a great way to enhance the learning experience for you and your students. Explore more at www.mrgrantmoney.com/music.
Thank you for allowing The Amazing Adventures of Mr. Grant Money to be a part of your educational journey. Together, let's unlock the doors to opportunity and success!

Best Regards,

Rodney

Grant Central USA

P.S. Be sure to visit our website and sign up for our newsletters to stay current.

The Amazing Adventures of
MR. GRANT MONEY

Journey To Acceptance:
Navigating College
Applications

VOLUME TWO

RODNEY WALKER

STRIVE press

Chief Editor: Laine Minerales
Editorial Assistant: Daniel Tuano
Production Supervisor: Joerje Galo
Electronic Composition: Jairus Agoncillo
Photographer: Studio 5404
Executive Marketing Manager: Jimmy Moore

Discover the breadth of our series, encompassing a myriad of crucial topics. Delve into the realms of grant acquisition, college scholarships, entrepreneurship, social impact, philanthropy, and beyond. Unearth a treasure trove of knowledge and empowerment within our diverse collection. Explore the wealth of insights awaiting you across these transformative series.

To inquire about utilizing The Amazing Adventures of Mr. Grant Money books in the classroom, securing licensing, and exploring special pricing for bulk orders, kindly contact us at info@grantcentralusa.com.

SBN: 979-8-89725-030-1 (Hardback)
ISBN: 979-8-89725-001-1 (Paperback)
ISBN: 979-8-89725-031-8 (Ebook)
ISBN: 979-8-89725-039-4 (Audiobook)

Printed in the United States

Dedication

This book is dedicated to the fighters—the ones who refuse to give up, no matter how hard the journey gets. To those who turn struggles into strength and obstacles into stepping stones.

You are proof that resilience can rewrite any story, and your determination can take you places others only dream of. Keep going, because the world needs your brilliance. I believe in you and can't wait to see you shine.

With love and appreciation,
Rodney

PREFACE

I will never forget the day I walked into my high school guidance counselor's office, eager to embrace the challenge of honors English. The summer had been spent in a relentless pursuit of knowledge, and I believed I was ready to take on the academic challenges that awaited me. Little did I know that this simple request would set the stage for a pivotal moment that would shape my trajectory through my senior year and beyond.

My counselor, perhaps fueled by a misguided notion, walked me down the hallway and gestured towards a nearly all-white honors English classroom. With a pointed question, she challenged my ability to compete with the students within. In that moment, my confidence wavered, and the doubt crept in. As a senior in my final year of high school, the seed of uncertainty took root. If my counselor questioned my readiness, maybe I wasn't up to the challenge.

Regrettably, I succumbed to that doubt and chose not to enroll in honors English. It marked the beginning of a phase where I stopped giving my best and started coasting through the remainder of my senior year, doing just enough to get by. Little did I realize the impact this decision would have on my direct path to the college of my choice. While I did eventually find my way to that desired college, the journey was not straightforward. I was uninformed about the college application process, and the entire endeavor felt like a maze with no guide to lead me through. I vividly remember the moment of embarrassment when a peer proudly announced her chosen college, and I found myself unable to answer the same question because I hadn't even applied.

It was this moment of realization, coupled with my own winding journey to college and later earning a Master's in Business Administration, that fueled a promise to myself. I vowed that when the time was right, I would do my part to help others navigate the complex terrain of college admissions and secure scholarships for a brighter future. This book is the fulfillment of that promise.

While there are countless books on scholarships and navigating the college landscape, I wanted to offer something different. Inspired by my own experiences, I sought to create a book that not only imparts practical knowledge but also inspires young readers to dream bigger. I want to encourage them with stories that stretch the imagination and showcase the boundless possibilities that education and perseverance can unlock.

As I reflect on that fateful day in the hallway, where uncertainty and embarrassment loomed large, I am grateful for the counselor whose words became the catalyst for this journey. In many ways, her doubts became the fuel that propelled me to excel, and now, with this book, I am committed to providing the guidance and inspiration I wish I had received.

To every young mind yearning for knowledge, every dreamer aspiring to greatness, and every individual navigating the intricate path to higher education, may this book be a beacon of hope and a source of invaluable scholarship success secrets.

With determination and dedication,

Rodney Walker

TABLE OF CONTENT

INTRODUCTION

In the glittering tapestry of Mr. Grant Money's adventures, there lies a journey that beckons not just the seeker of knowledge but the dreamer of acceptance. Imagine stepping into a world where wisdom dances in the air, elegance adorns every thought, and philanthropy is the compass guiding each step. As you open the pages of "The Amazing Adventures of Mr. Grant Money Vol. 2: Journey To Acceptance: Navigating College Applications," prepare to be captivated by tales that transcend the mundane and elevate the pursuit of higher education to a symphony of insight, elegance, and transformation.

Why should you delve into these pages, you might ask? Because within them, you'll find not just stories, but keys to unlock the doors of acceptance. Each narrative is a map, charting the course through the intricate journey of college applications. Picture yourself strolling through the vibrant streets of Los Angeles, standing in the heart of Silicon Valley's innovation, or gazing at the monumental destiny that is Washington, D.C. These settings are not just backdrops but stages for the timeless lessons awaiting you.

Our purpose here is clear – to guide, inspire, and empower. This isn't just a book; it's a companion on your expedition to acceptance. With engaging exercises, word puzzles to stimulate your mind, success stories to fuel your aspirations, and questions to provoke thoughtful discussions, this book extends an invitation to an active participation in your own narrative.

As you immerse yourself in Mr. Grant Money's world, expect vivid language that paints images in your mind, creating an immersive experience that lingers. The tone resonates with the heartbeat of each story, whether it's the suspense of a college essay rewrite, the elegance of a boutique in Los Angeles, or the intrigue of Silicon Valley's untold paths.

Meet key characters – not just on the pages but in your journey. From the enchanting streets of Boston to the sprawling landscapes of Houston, characters emerge, sharing wisdom, facing challenges, and leaving an indelible mark on the narrative canvas. Feel the tension, the conflict – the very essence that propels you forward, turning pages eagerly to uncover resolutions and revelations.

But let's not reveal too much. The mystery lies in the untold, and as you navigate these initial pages, you'll find yourself drawn into a world where acceptance is not just a destination but a transformative journey.

So, with a taste of what's to come, let the adventure unfold. The introduction is merely the overture; the symphony of acceptance awaits as you step into the main narrative, guided by the wisdom, elegance, and philanthropy of Mr. Grant Money's remarkable journey.

The Amazing Adventures of
MRGRANTMONEY
WAVES OF WISDOM

Golden Waves of Wisdom: Mr. Grant Money's College Compass

Dive Into The Azure Depths Of Scholarship Challenges With Mr. Grant Money. As Waves Of Insight Crash Upon Him.

Mr. Grant Money woke up in the lap of luxury, surrounded by the turquoise waters of Bora Bora at a five-star resort. As he stepped onto his private terrace, he looked out at the pristine beach and lush greenery, taking in the beauty of the paradise around him. With a grin on his face, he declared to himself, "Today is a great day to make a great day!"

Dressed in his usual stylish attire, Mr. Grant Money made his way to the resort's elegant dining area for breakfast. The atmosphere was enchanting, with the scent of tropical flowers lingering in the air and the gentle sound of waves in the background. As he sipped his herbal tea and enjoyed a delicious spread, flashes of insight hit his mind like rays of sunshine breaking through the palm fronds.

Several ideas sprang into Mr. Grant Money's mind, all centered around helping young people achieve greater success with scholarships. However, amidst these thoughts, he realized that winning scholarships was only one part of the journey. Another critical aspect was navigating the path to college itself.

Reflecting on his own high school days, Mr. Grant Money recalled the challenges he faced in finding guidance and direction. Determined to make a difference, he headed to the beach with his trusty Golden Journal. As the waves gently kissed the shore, he jotted down a few notes and contacted Maximus, a member of his Power House Crew to conduct extensive research on the top challenges students face when trying to navigate the path to college.

The list he sent him outlined ten major challenges:

1. Financial Barriers:
 - Difficulty in affording the cost of tuition, books, and living expenses.

2. Academic Pressure:
 - Balancing a challenging academic workload and maintaining a competitive GPA.

3. Standardized Testing Stress:
 - Preparing for and performing well on standardized tests such as the SAT or ACT.

4. College Selection Dilemma:
 - Choosing the right college that aligns with academic and personal goals.

5. Application Process Complexity:
 - Navigating through the complex college application process, including essays and recommendation letters.

6. Competition for Scholarships:
 - Facing intense competition for scholarships and financial aid.

7. Transition and Adjustment:
 - Adapting to the new environment and lifestyle, especially for students moving away from home.

8. Career and Major Indecision:
 - Uncertainty about career goals and choosing a suitable major.

9. Time Management:
 - Juggling academics, extracurricular activities, part-time work, and personal life.

10. Mental Health Struggles:
 - Coping with stress, anxiety, and the overall mental health challenges associated with the college journey.

Reading through the list, Mr. Grant Money recognized the struggles he had faced when he was in high school. Squeezing his scepter in contemplation, the idea of organizing the MGM Scholarship Success Summit struck him like lightning. Excitedly, he instructed his team to plan an event that he could take to various cities annually.

With unwavering determination, Mr. Grant Money aimed to provide valuable insights to students facing these challenges. He envisioned a platform where experts could guide and inspire them, ensuring every student had a chance at success. The summit would cover everything from financial literacy to stress management, offering a holistic approach to overcoming obstacles.

Closing his Golden Journal with a triumphant smile, Mr. Grant Money uttered, "Making a difference is what life is all about." With plans in place, he knew that the future would be brighter for countless students. As he returned to enjoy the idyllic surroundings of Bora Bora, he reveled in the knowledge that he was leaving a lasting impact on the lives of those striving for a better education and a brighter future.

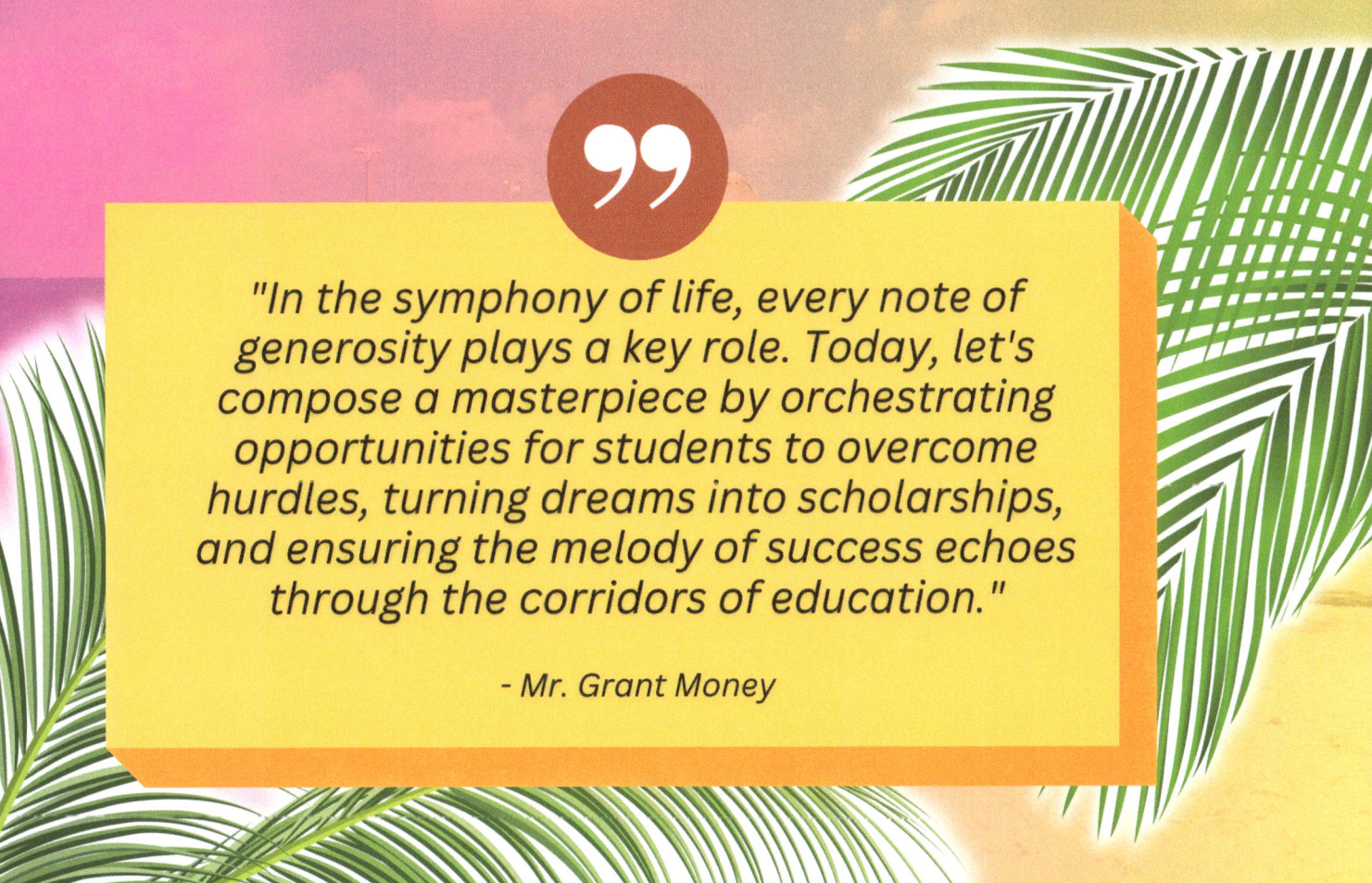

"In the symphony of life, every note of generosity plays a key role. Today, let's compose a masterpiece by orchestrating opportunities for students to overcome hurdles, turning dreams into scholarships, and ensuring the melody of success echoes through the corridors of education."

- Mr. Grant Money

Exercise: "Navigating the College Journey Game Plan"

Objective: The goal of this exercise is to empower students to self-identify challenges they may face in navigating their way to college and develop a proactive game plan to overcome these challenges.

Materials Needed:
1. Pen/pencil
2. Paper or notebook
3. Access to online resources (optional)

Instructions:

1. Reflection (15 minutes):
- Ask students to find a quiet space and reflect on their current situation regarding their journey to college. Encourage them to consider academic, financial, and personal aspects. Have them jot down any challenges or concerns that come to mind.

2. Identify Challenges (15 minutes):
- Have students create a list of challenges they've identified in their notebooks. Encourage them to be honest and specific. This could include issues related to academics, standardized testing, financial barriers, college selection, application processes, or personal well-being.

3. Group Discussion (20 minutes):
- Form small groups and have students share their identified challenges with their group members. This provides an opportunity for peer support and the exchange of ideas.

4. Game Plan Development (30 minutes):
- Ask each student to develop a proactive game plan to address their identified challenges. In their notebooks, prompt them to consider the following:

- What resources are available to help overcome these challenges?
- Can specific people, such as teachers, counselors, or family members, provide guidance or support?
- What steps can they take in the short term to alleviate these challenges?
- How can they prioritize and manage their time effectively?

5. Share and Discuss Game Plans (15 minutes):
- Invite students to share their game plans with the class or their small groups. Encourage a discussion about different strategies and solutions. Emphasize the importance of proactive and positive approaches to overcoming challenges.

6. Reflection and Goal Setting (10 minutes):
- Ask students to reflect on what they've learned during the exercise. Have them set realistic and achievable short-term goals based on their game plans. Encourage them to revisit and revise these goals regularly.

7. Follow-Up (Ongoing):
- Encourage students to revisit their game plans periodically and make adjustments as needed. Provide ongoing support and resources, such as information on scholarships, workshops, or counseling services, to help them navigate their journey to college successfully.

This exercise aims to foster self-awareness, proactive problem-solving, and a sense of empowerment among students as they navigate the challenges on their path to higher education.

"Just as the sun rises over Bora Bora, so too can the dawn of knowledge dispel the shadows of ignorance. Empowering students isn't just about writing checks; it's about illuminating the path to success, guiding them through the challenges, and letting the radiance of education shine in every corner of their lives."

- Mr. Grant Money

Discussion Questions

1. What inspired Mr. Grant Money to focus specifically on helping students overcome challenges in their journey to college, and how did his own experiences shape this philanthropic vision?

2. In organizing the MGM Scholarship Success Summit, Mr. Grant Money aims to address a wide range of challenges faced by students. Which of the ten challenges outlined do you think is the most critical for students today, and why?

3. Discuss the significance of incorporating a holistic approach in the summit, covering topics from financial literacy to stress management. How might addressing these diverse aspects contribute to a more successful college journey for students?

4. Mr. Grant Money emphasizes the importance of making a difference in the lives of students striving for a better education. In your opinion, how can initiatives like the MGM Scholarship Success Summit impact not only individuals but also communities and society as a whole?

5. Considering the luxurious setting of Bora Bora where Mr. Grant Money had his moment of inspiration, do you think the opulence of the environment influenced his decision to focus on scholarship and education initiatives? How might the setting shape the way philanthropists approach their charitable endeavors?

 Big Idea "The MGM Mentorship Network"

Recognizing the importance of personalized guidance, Mr. Grant Money could establish a mentorship network connecting successful professionals, alumni, and educators with students facing challenges in their journey to college. This network would provide one-on-one mentorship, offering guidance on academics, career choices, and personal development. To enhance accessibility, the mentorship program could utilize online platforms, allowing students to connect with mentors regardless of their location. Additionally, the MGM Mentorship Network could organize periodic networking events, fostering a sense of community and creating opportunities for students to learn from real-world experiences.

🔍 Word Search

Embark on an exciting word search puzzle adventure inspired by the captivating story of Mr. Grant Money's luxurious day in paradise. As he soaked in the beauty of Bora Bora, a burst of inspiration led him to envision the MGM Scholarship Success Summit, a groundbreaking initiative to help students overcome challenges on their journey to college.

Immerse yourself in the world of Mr. Grant Money's vision as you search the words related to scholarships, education, and success.

Now, here are the 15 words for the word search puzzle based on the story:

C	S	E	G	N	E	L	L	A	H	C	R	R	I
C	T	S	I	I	F	C	M	O	I	N	I	S	I
E	T	C	E	A	I	E	N	N	G	O	N	T	I
C	I	H	Y	E	N	R	U	O	J	I	T	D	D
O	E	O	H	S	A	C	C	I	A	T	A	I	E
M	C	L	P	U	N	M	G	T	N	A	C	F	S
P	N	A	M	C	C	C	D	A	S	C	A	F	I
E	A	R	U	C	I	U	T	R	T	U	D	E	D
T	D	S	I	E	A	L	T	I	R	D	E	R	A
I	I	H	R	S	L	I	U	P	U	E	M	E	R
T	U	I	T	S	M	H	P	S	G	O	I	N	A
I	G	P	S	M	A	T	S	N	G	D	C	C	P
O	S	U	U	R	D	N	O	I	L	U	L	E	E
N	C	S	H	R	N	I	P	S	E	A	T	D	I

FINANCIAL
INSPIRATION
EDUCATION
DIFFERENCE
GUIDANCE
SCHOLARSHIP
SUMMIT
ACADEMIC
CHALLENGES
STRUGGLE
SUCCESS
TRIUMPH
COMPETITION
PARADISE
JOURNEY

"Education is the compass that guides us through the uncharted waters of our potential. As we strive to make a difference, let's remember that the true measure of success lies not just in personal achievements but in the positive impact we make on the journeys of others, particularly those seeking the shores of knowledge."

SUCCESS STORIES

"Sophie's Scholarship Triumph: A Journey from Small Town Dreams to Community Impact"

Sophie Summers, a small-town dreamer, found inspiration in the success story of Mr. Grant Money, waking up in luxury in Bora Bora. Fueled by determination, she faced the familiar challenges of financial barriers and academic pressure. The whispers of success seemed distant, but Sophie, echoing Mr. Grant Money's mantra, believed that today was a great day to make a great day.

As Sophie navigated high school, she encountered setbacks, including financial barriers and the stress of standardized testing. Undeterred, she formed her makeshift Power House Crew, seeking support from mentors and teachers. Late-night study sessions and tears became her companions, but Sophie learned from each failure, turning setbacks into stepping stones towards success.

Inspired by Mr. Grant Money's MGM Scholarship Success Summit, Sophie decided to organize a similar event in her community. Rallying teachers, local leaders, and fellow students, she created a platform addressing challenges such as financial barriers, academic pressures, and career indecision. The summit not only transformed Sophie's life but became a beacon of hope for her community, spreading inspiration and solutions to aspiring students.

Sophie's journey, much like Mr. Grant Money's, embodied the spirit of making a difference. Standing on the summit stage, surrounded by aspiring students, she realized the delicious dish of success wasn't reserved for the privileged few. It was a feast for anyone with determination, resilience, and the belief that today is a great day to make a great day. Sophie's story became a testament to the transformative power of perseverance and community impact, leaving a lasting legacy in the small town she called home.

BEYOND THE PAGES

The Amazing Adventures of
MRGRANTMONEY

Beyond the Pages: Mr. Grant Money's Boston Odyssey

A Tale Of Inspiration, Scholarship, And The Power Of Libraries

Mr. Grant Money arrived in Boston in style, ready to make a difference in the iconic city library. Dressed impeccably in a tailored suit that radiated confidence, he stepped onto the stage with an air of charisma that instantly captured the attention of the students and educators gathered for the Scholarship Success Summit.

Mr. Grant Money engaged the audience with his warm and dynamic personality as he began his presentation. His stylish attire complemented the grandeur of the library's surroundings, creating a captivating scene for the students eager to absorb valuable insights.

Surrounded by towering shelves of books, Mr. Grant Money explained the process of researching colleges and gathering information. He emphasized the symbolic significance of the library setting, encouraging students to view the wealth of knowledge around them as a metaphor for the vast resources available when exploring their academic and career paths.

With enthusiasm, Mr. Grant Money highlighted the importance of utilizing both online and offline resources in the research process.

He encouraged students to dive into books, academic journals, and online databases to comprehensively understand potential colleges, majors, and career options. The rows of books served as a visual representation of the multitude of possibilities awaiting exploration.

In his dialogue with the students and educators, Mr. Grant Money stressed the value of seeking guidance from librarians and college counselors. He shared anecdotes from his own journey, underscoring the impact of mentorship and expert advice in shaping his successful path. The library's hallowed halls became a symbolic space for exchanging ideas and pursuing knowledge.

As Mr. Grant Money concluded his presentation, the students and educators rose to their feet, giving him a standing ovation. He acknowledged the applause with a gracious smile and uttered, "I've done the easy part; now it is time for you to work your magic by taking action."

Leaving the audience inspired and motivated, Mr. Grant Money exited the library with a sense of accomplishment. As he stepped into the bustling streets of Boston, he couldn't help but wonder where his next wondrous adventure would lead him.

The city library had set the stage for transformative conversations, and Mr. Grant Money was eager to continue his mission of positively impacting the educational journeys of students across the country.

"In the vast library of life, every book holds a chapter of opportunity. Research with passion, study with purpose, and write your success story with determination."

- Mr. Grant Money

Exercise: "Independent College Research Exploration"

Objective: This exercise is designed to empower students to take the initiative in researching colleges and gathering information independently. It can be implemented by either the student on their own or guided by a teacher as part of a classroom activity.

Materials Needed:
1. Pen/pencil
2. Notebook or paper
3. Access to computers/tablets for online research
4. Library resources (if conducted on-site)

Instructions:

1. Goal Setting (10 minutes):
- If led by a teacher: Begin by discussing the importance of independent college research and goal-setting. Encourage students to think about their academic and career aspirations.
- If done independently: Set personal goals for the research, outlining what the student hopes to discover and achieve through the process.

2. Resource Introduction (10 minutes):
- Explore online resources, college websites, and forums that may be valuable for research. Take note of any potential leads for further investigation.

3. Library Exploration (30 minutes - On-site or as Homework):
- Visit the library independently, focusing on resources related to colleges and careers. Take notes on interesting findings and potential colleges that align with personal goals.

4. Online Research (30 minutes):
- Conduct online research, exploring college websites, forums, and educational portals. Gather information on majors offered, admission requirements, campus life, and alumni success stories.

5. Compilation and Reflection (20 minutes):

- Reflect on the information gathered, noting any discoveries and personal insights. Compile the findings for future reference.

6. Action Plan (15 minutes):

- Develop a personal action plan outlining specific, achievable goals for ongoing college exploration. Consider steps to take in the near future based on the research.

7. Reflection and Evaluation (15 minutes):

- If done independently: Reflect on the research process and evaluate the effectiveness of the resources used. Consider sharing insights with peers, teachers, or mentors.

This exercise aims to instill a sense of independence and initiative in students as they embark on their college research journey. Whether guided by a teacher or undertaken independently, the goal is to encourage proactive exploration and thoughtful reflection.

"Just as these books surround us, knowledge envelops you. Navigate the shelves of your ambitions, consult the librarians of experience, and draft the chapters of your future with the ink of relentless effort."

- Mr. Grant Money

Discussion Questions

1. How did Mr. Grant Money effectively use the symbolic setting of the iconic city library to convey his message about the importance of research, knowledge, and exploration in the academic and career journey of students?

2. In what ways did Mr. Grant Money's emphasis on utilizing both online and offline resources for college and career research resonate with the audience, and how might this dual approach contribute to a more comprehensive understanding for students?

3. The story highlights Mr. Grant Money's emphasis on seeking guidance from librarians and college counselors. How do you think mentorship and expert advice, as illustrated by Mr. Grant Money's anecdotes, can impact the success of students in their educational pursuits?

4. The standing ovation at the end of Mr. Grant Money's presentation suggests a strong positive response from the audience. What elements of his presentation do you think were most effective in capturing the attention and inspiring the students and educators in attendance?

5. Mr. Grant Money stated, "I've done the easy part; now it is time for you to work your magic by taking action." What actions do you think students can take to translate the inspiration and motivation they gained from Mr. Grant Money's presentation into tangible steps for their own educational journeys?

 Big Idea "The Virtual Scholarship Success Summit"

Building upon the success of Mr. Grant Money's engaging presentation at the Scholarship Success Summit, an innovative event could be developed: the Virtual Scholarship Success Summit. This online platform would enable students from around the country to attend a series of presentations, workshops, and interactive sessions led by influential figures in education, career counseling, and scholarship management. By leveraging virtual reality or immersive online platforms, students could experience the summit from the comfort of their homes while still benefiting from the captivating atmosphere that inspired them during Mr. Grant Money's visit to the Boston library. The summit could provide a dynamic space for knowledge exchange, networking, and inspiration on a national scale.

🔍 Word Search

Embark on a literary journey inspired by the charismatic Mr. Grant Money, who graced the iconic city library in Boston with his presence. Dressed in a tailored suit that radiated confidence, Mr. Grant Money captivated the audience at the Scholarship Success Summit with his warm and dynamic personality.

Surrounded by the grandeur of the library's towering shelves of books, he shared invaluable insights on researching colleges and emphasized the symbolic significance of the rich knowledge repository around.

Now, here are the 15 words for the word search puzzle based on the story:

T	R	U	E	M	T	N	A	R	G	O	C	M	E
O	L	R	U	R	E	R	U	T	N	E	V	D	A
E	S	C	S	N	E	G	D	E	L	W	O	N	K
P	B	O	S	T	O	N	R	M	A	J	O	R	S
G	U	I	D	A	N	C	E	C	T	E	I	U	C
N	M	S	U	C	C	E	S	S	S	Y	N	C	A
A	S	E	M	I	S	N	T	H	Y	M	C	E	R
S	U	S	C	H	O	L	A	R	S	H	I	P	E
M	U	S	S	E	I	R	A	C	R	S	U	T	E
R	O	P	I	H	S	R	O	T	N	E	M	L	R
E	S	N	N	P	B	S	E	G	E	L	L	O	C
R	S	C	E	I	H	C	R	A	E	S	E	R	S
S	D	A	L	Y	N	M	R	B	E	O	H	E	A
U	C	S	L	M	S	H	S	U	M	M	I	T	L

CAREER
SCHOLARSHIP
SUCCESS
MONEY
LIBRARY
MAJORS
ADVENTURE
SUMMIT
BOSTON
GRANT
KNOWLEDGE
RESEARCH
GUIDANCE
COLLEGES
MENTORSHIP

"Amidst the towering shelves of wisdom, Mr. Grant Money illuminated a path of knowledge, reminding us that the library of dreams is open to those who dare to explore. In the silent whispers of pages and the echoes of applause, the city library echoed the boundless potential within each student's journey."

SUCCESS STORIES

"The Harmonious Triumph: Kara's Symphony of Success in the Heart of Boston"

In the heart of Boston, where the cobblestone streets resonate with history and the skyscrapers reach for the sky, there lived a young woman named Kara. Her life, much like the city itself, was a blend of the old and the new, the tried and the true, and the bold and the innovative. Kara's story, akin to a symphony, was a melodic journey of triumph and perseverance, where each instrument represented a pivotal chapter in her life, harmonizing into a crescendo of achievement.

The violin in this symphony was Kara's passion. It sang with a delicate yet intense fervor, mirroring her early struggles and her fierce determination. She was like a soloist, playing her heart out in the midst of chaos, each stroke symbolizing her relentless efforts to overcome the challenges of her upbringing in the bustling city.

The piano, with its resonant and versatile notes, represented Kara's education. Each key was a step in her academic journey, played with precision and grace. The melody it produced was one of enlightenment and growth, echoing through the hallowed halls of Boston's libraries and classrooms, where she spent countless hours honing her intellect.

The trumpet, bold and triumphant, symbolized Kara's breakthrough moments. Just as a trumpet announces victory or celebration, each of Kara's achievements rang out clear and strong. This was the instrument of her successes, from receiving scholarships to gaining recognition for her community work.

The drums, the backbone of any symphony, were Kara's resilience. They boomed with the rhythm of her unyielding spirit, never letting the symphony lose its pace or purpose. Even when faced with setbacks, the drums kept beating, pushing the melody forward, embodying Kara's tenacity.

And then there was the harp, ethereal and often in the background, representing the support and love of her family and friends. Its gentle strums provided a comforting undertone to Kara's life, reminding her that she was not alone in her journey.

In the grand hall of life, where Kara's symphony played, there was a day that stood out. It was the day Mr. Grant Money came to the Boston City Library for the Scholarship Success Summit. Kara, among the audience, was captivated by his presence and words. He spoke not just of scholarships and academics, but of life's grand pursuit of knowledge and purpose.

As Mr. Grant Money's speech concluded and the crowd erupted in applause, Kara felt a surge of inspiration. His words resonated with her, much like the instruments in her symphony. She realized that her journey, her symphony, was not just about her struggles or her triumphs, but about how beautifully they all came together to create a melody that was uniquely hers.

Months and years passed, and Kara's symphony grew richer, more complex. She became a beacon of hope and inspiration in her community, much like Mr. Grant Money had been for her. Her story was not just about a girl from Boston who overcame odds; it was about how each aspect of her life, each instrument in her symphony, played a crucial role in harmonizing her path to success.

As the final notes of her symphony echoed, Kara stood in the very library where she had once been an awestruck listener. Now, she was the speaker, the mentor, the inspiration. Her story, like the most beautiful symphonies, became timeless – a testament to the power of resilience, education, passion, and support. In the heart of Boston, Kara's symphony played on, an everlasting melody of success and hope.

Beyond Skyscrapers: Mr. Grant Money's Academic Ascent in Houston

Cheating The System? A Texan Tale Of Lessons Learned

Mr. Grant Money found himself in the heart of Houston, Texas, a city known for its towering skyscrapers, cultural diversity, and vibrant energy. Excited to explore the major landmarks, he strolled through Hermann Park, marveled at the Space Center Houston, and admired the breathtaking skyline. As he soaked in the Texan atmosphere, Mr. Grant Money couldn't help but be inspired by the mantra that everything is indeed bigger in Texas.

With this idea in mind, he headed to a charter school in Houston, where he was invited to speak to a group of motivated students. The school, nestled in a bustling neighborhood, exuded a sense of enthusiasm and ambition. Mr. Grant Money, as always, was impeccably dressed, radiating confidence and warmth as he addressed the eager audience.

"Hey there, Houston! They say everything's bigger in Texas, right?" Mr. Grant Money began with a grin. The students chuckled and nodded in agreement.

"Well, here's a big idea for you all: Go big when it comes to your efforts in getting into the right college for you," he declared, his voice echoing through the auditorium. "But remember, going big doesn't mean trying to cheat the process. Trust me; I've learned that lesson the hard way."

Mr. Grant Money proceeded to share a personal story from his high school days, specifically his 12th-grade English class with Mrs. Richardson. Every Friday, the class had a vocabulary test, and to save time, papers were passed to the person in front or back for grading. It was a system that seemed convenient until Mr. Grant Money and his friend decided to cut corners.

"We thought we were clever, filling in each other's answers to ensure good grades. And it worked for a while," he admitted with a chuckle, but the room fell silent as he continued. "Until one Friday, Mrs. Richardson decided to stand right next to us while giving the correct answers. We couldn't cheat without her noticing. Needless to say, we both got low grades that week."

The audience listened attentively, sensing the gravity of the lesson being shared. Mr. Grant Money continued, "But the real kicker came later, during the SAT. As I stared at the test, I noticed the same words I'd seen on Mrs. Richardson's quizzes. I realized you can't cheat the process in the long run. You've got to go big and put in the work required to succeed."

The students nodded in understanding, absorbing the wisdom Mr. Grant Money was imparting. He concluded his talk with a powerful quote, "In the grand scheme of things, shortcuts only lead to dead ends. Trust the process, go big, and success will be bigger than you ever imagined."

As Mr. Grant Money left the charter school, he felt a sense of fulfillment, knowing that he had inspired the students to embrace the journey ahead. With the Texan sun setting behind him, he continued his exploration of Houston, eager to discover more of the city's grandeur and share his lessons with students across the country.

"In the vast landscape of life, shortcuts may seem tempting, but remember, the truest triumphs are born from the monumental efforts you invest. Trust the process, my friends, and watch your success rise taller than the towering skyscrapers of Texas."

- Mr. Grant Money

Exercise: "The College Journey Reflection"

Objective: The goal of this exercise is to guide students in reflecting on their personal journey towards college, emphasizing the importance of trusting the process and avoiding shortcuts. The exercise is designed to encourage self-awareness, goal-setting, and a commitment to the hard work required for long-term success.

Materials Needed:
1. Pen/pencil
2. Notebook or paper

Instructions:

1. Introduction (10 minutes):
- Begin by discussing the importance of the college journey and the impact of decisions made during high school. Introduce the concept of trusting the process and avoiding shortcuts, using Mr. Grant Money's story as an example.

2. Personal Reflection (20 minutes):
- Ask students to take some time to reflect on their own journey towards college. In their notebooks, encourage them to answer the following questions:

- What are my current goals for college and beyond?
- Have I encountered challenges or temptations to take shortcuts in my academic journey?
- How have I overcome obstacles or made decisions to stay on the right path?
- What lessons can I learn from Mr. Grant Money's story?

3. Group Discussion (15 minutes):
- Form small groups and have students share their reflections with their peers. Encourage open discussions about common challenges, strategies for overcoming obstacles, and the importance of setting realistic goals.

4. Goal-Setting (20 minutes):
- Guide students in setting specific, achievable goals for the upcoming months or academic year. Emphasize the importance of aligning these goals with their long-term aspirations. Encourage them to consider academic, extracurricular, and personal development goals.

5. Action Plan (15 minutes):

- Instruct students to develop a practical action plan to achieve their goals. This plan should include specific steps, resources they will utilize, and a timeline for completion. Emphasize the idea of "going big" in their efforts to achieve these goals.

6. Sharing and Feedback (15 minutes):

- Encourage students to share their goals and action plans with the class. Provide constructive feedback and insights to their peers. Emphasize the importance of supporting each other on their respective journeys.

7. Reflection and Commitment (10 minutes):

- Conclude the exercise with a final reflection. Ask students to write a brief summary of what they've learned from the exercise and how they plan to commit to their goals, trusting the process and avoiding shortcuts.

Homework/Extended Activity (Optional):

- Assign a follow-up assignment where students write a personal essay or create a vision board that represents their long-term goals and commitment to the college journey.

This exercise aims to foster self-reflection, goal-setting, and a commitment to the hard work required for success. By drawing inspiration from Mr. Grant Money's story, students can internalize the importance of trusting the process and making thoughtful decisions on their educational paths.

"Life's SAT test is filled with challenges that echo the lessons of our past. Attempting to cheat the journey may grant temporary victories, but it's the honest effort that writes the enduring narrative of success. Go big, stay true, and let the echoes of your hard work resonate louder than the Texan cheers at a football game."

TEXAS

Discussion Questions

1. Reflecting on Mr. Grant Money's personal experience, do you think there are situations where taking shortcuts might seem tempting, but in the long run, they hinder success rather than contribute to it? Can you share any personal anecdotes or examples that support or challenge this idea?

2. In his talk, Mr. Grant Money emphasized the importance of "going big" in efforts to achieve one's goals, particularly in the context of pursuing the right college. How do you interpret the concept of "going big" in your own life and aspirations? What strategies do you think can help someone pursue their goals with dedication and commitment?

3. Mr. Grant Money shared a pivotal moment during his high school days when he and a friend attempted to cheat the system but ultimately faced consequences. How do you think experiences, both positive and negative, shape our understanding of success and the value of hard work? Can you think of any experiences in your own life that have influenced your perspective on success and achievement?

4. The talk concluded with Mr. Grant Money encouraging the students to trust the process and avoid shortcuts. How can one strike a balance between being ambitious and patient in their pursuit of success? Are there instances in your own life where patience and perseverance have played a crucial role in achieving a goal?

5. Mr. Grant Money's journey of self-discovery during the SAT, realizing that the words on the test were the same as those on Mrs. Richardson's quizzes, highlighted the interconnectedness of learning experiences. How do you think the lessons we learn in various aspects of life contribute to our overall growth and success? Can you identify any unexpected connections between different areas of your own learning and development?

 Big Idea "The "Go Big" College Prep Program"

Build a comprehensive college preparation program that encourages students to aim high and put in the necessary effort. This program could include workshops, mentorship opportunities, and resources that guide students through the college application process, standardized testing, essay writing, and interview skills. Emphasize the importance of genuine effort and personal growth, steering them away from shortcuts and unethical practices. Partner with schools and organizations to implement this program and make it accessible to students nationwide.

🔍 Word Search

Welcome to the "Mr. Grant Money Word Search Puzzle," inspired by the adventures of the charismatic Mr. Grant Money in the heart of Houston, Texas! Join Mr. Grant Money as he explores the vibrant city, shares valuable lessons with ambitious students, and imparts the wisdom that success is achieved by going big and trusting the process.

Now, let's dive into the puzzle and discover the words related to Mr. Grant Money's journey and the life-changing lesson he learned in Houston.

Now, here are the 15 words for the word search puzzle based on the story:

R	T	N	E	G	E	L	L	O	C	R	E	E	E
T	K	P	N	S	A	P	H	E	I	S	C	L	O
E	L	I	S	A	A	S	N	O	T	A	N	N	A
M	N	Y	A	O	M	I	T	N	P	M	R	O	E
Y	S	E	P	R	L	R	K	S	L	B	S	I	R
T	E	I	R	Y	T	T	E	N	I	I	I	T	H
I	O	E	K	G	R	N	L	H	E	T	A	A	R
S	N	S	R	N	Y	T	A	A	T	I	S	R	A
R	R	N	E	O	B	R	T	M	H	O	R	I	P
E	I	O	T	N	C	H	E	T	T	N	I	P	A
V	T	S	N	P	R	E	F	F	O	R	T	S	R
I	N	S	E	H	O	U	S	T	O	N	E	N	K
D	E	E	C	F	P	Y	A	I	T	G	I	I	C
E	S	L	S	K	Y	S	C	R	A	P	E	R	S

COLLEGE
CENTER
SKYLINE
ENERGY
AMBITION
EFFORTS
LESSON
DIVERSITY
SPACE
PARK
SKYSCRAPERS
HERMANN
MANTRA
INSPIRATION
HOUSTON

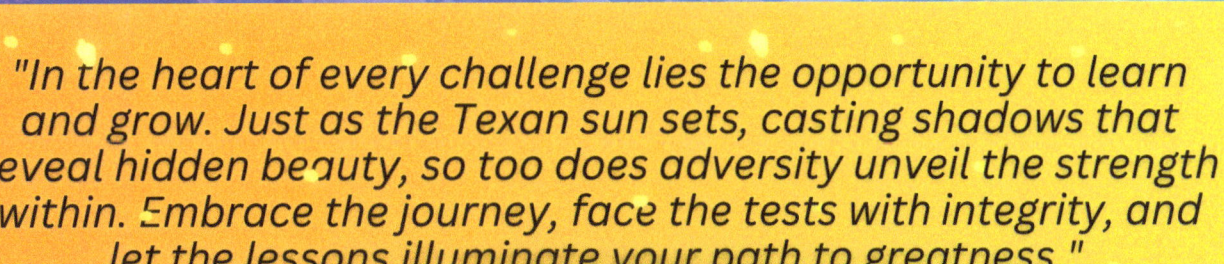

"In the heart of every challenge lies the opportunity to learn and grow. Just as the Texan sun sets, casting shadows that reveal hidden beauty, so too does adversity unveil the strength within. Embrace the journey, face the tests with integrity, and let the lessons illuminate your path to greatness."

SUCCESS STORIES

"From Shortcuts to Success: Gerald's Transformative Journey of Hard Work and Integrity in the Heart of Houston"

In the bustling city of Houston, Texas, Gerald, a high school student, found himself at a turning point. During a speech at his school by Mr. Grant Money, a renowned speaker, Gerald was struck by a story about the pitfalls of taking shortcuts in life. This moment ignited a change in Gerald, leading him to abandon the lure of quick wins in favor of hard work and dedication.

Motivated by Mr. Money's speech, Gerald transformed his approach to academics and extracurricular activities. He devoted extra hours to studying, even in subjects he found challenging, and actively participated in school clubs and projects. This shift in mindset led to a remarkable improvement in his grades and recognition from teachers and peers alike.

Gerald's commitment and hard work paid off as he excelled in his SATs and received multiple college acceptance letters, including from prestigious universities that once seemed out of reach. His achievements were not just academic; Gerald had undergone a profound personal growth, developing resilience and an appreciation for the value of perseverance and integrity.

Years later, as a successful professional and university alumnus, Gerald often reflected on the impact of Mr. Grant Money's speech. It was a pivotal moment that taught him the true essence of success — not just in achieving goals but in the journey and personal development that accompany them.

Gerald's story became an inspirational tale, not just for his immediate circle but for future generations of students. It served as a powerful reminder of the importance of hard work, integrity, and the transformative power of embracing challenges head-on in the pursuit of one's dreams.

BEYOND END ZONE

The Amazing Adventures of MRGRANTMONEY

Beyond End Zones: The Enduring Touchdown of College Success

Mr. Grant Money's Journey Through Pittsburgh Unveils The Secrets Of Long-Term Thinking

Mr. Grant Money, adorned in his signature impeccable attire, found himself immersed in the vibrant energy of Pittsburgh, a city known for its steel history, cultural richness, and bustling business scene. His visit to the Steel City involved exploring the iconic landmarks and soaking in the dynamic atmosphere that surrounded him.

Amidst the towering skyscrapers and bustling streets, Mr. Grant Money couldn't resist visiting some of Pittsburgh's main attractions. From the picturesque views atop Mount Washington to the lively atmosphere at the Strip District, he reveled in the diverse experiences the city had to offer.

As he wandered through the streets, Mr. Grant Money unexpectedly found himself passing by the campus of the University of Pittsburgh. The sight triggered a flood of memories, especially the image of his all-time favorite football player, Tony Dorsett. With a nostalgic smile, he recalled the day he had the privilege of meeting the legendary running back while strolling down a sunny California street.

The memories flashed vividly, with Mr. Grant Money recalling Tony Dorsett's famous long touchdown run—the kind of play that began in his own end zone and turned into a coast-to-coast spectacle of skill and determination.

With Tony Dorsett's electrifying run in mind, Mr. Grant Money transitioned into a story about the parallels between long-term thinking and short-term approaches in navigating the path to college.

Long-Term Thinking vs. Short-Term Approaches: Navigating the Path to College

1. Starting Early
- **Long-Term Thinking**: Students who adopt a long-term perspective on their college journey begin the preparation process early. This includes exploring potential majors, building a strong academic foundation, and participating in extracurricular activities that align with their interests.
- **Short-Term Approaches**: Those adopting short-term approaches may delay crucial steps in the college preparation process, missing out on valuable opportunities and experiences.

2. Sustained Efforts
- **Long-Term Thinking**: Students committed to long-term success recognize the importance of sustained efforts. They consistently invest time and energy into academic excellence, extracurricular activities, and community involvement.
- **Short-Term Approaches**: Taking shortcuts or relying on last-minute efforts may yield immediate results but often lack the depth and consistency required for long-term success.

3. Goal Alignment
- **Long-Term Thinking**: Students with a long-term mindset align their goals with their passions and career aspirations. This strategic alignment ensures that every step taken contributes to their overall vision for the future.
- **Short-Term Approaches**: Without a clear long-term vision, students may adopt short-term goals that lack coherence and fail to contribute to a comprehensive plan for their educational journey.

4. Resilience and Adaptability
- **Long-Term Thinking**: Students with a long-term perspective understand that setbacks are a natural part of the journey. They develop resilience and adaptability, learning from challenges and using them as opportunities for growth.

Short-Term Approaches: Individuals relying on short-term strategies may struggle to overcome obstacles, viewing setbacks as insurmountable roadblocks rather than opportunities for personal development.

As Mr. Grant Money concluded his reflections on the importance of long-term thinking, he felt a renewed sense of purpose.

He reached for his Golden Journal, clutching his Shirley Scepter, and jotted down the key points. The golden pages held the wisdom of countless stories and lessons, each entry a testament to the power of strategic thinking and sustained effort.

With a final glance back at the campus and the memories of Tony Dorsett's coast-to-coast run, Mr. Grant Money continued forward to his next journey, knowing that the lessons shared would inspire students to adopt a mindset that transcends short-term gains in favor of the enduring success that comes with long-term thinking.

"In the symphony of success, the notes of long-term thinking compose a masterpiece. Like Tony Dorsett's iconic run, the journey from end zone to career pinnacle requires strategic planning and sustained effort."
- *Mr. Grant Money*

Exercise: "Vision Board - Navigating the Path to College"

Objective: The objective of this exercise is to guide students in visualizing their long-term goals and adopting a strategic mindset for navigating the path to college. The creation of a vision board serves as a tangible representation of their aspirations, fostering a sense of motivation and purpose.

Materials Needed:
1. Magazines, newspapers, or printed images
2. Scissors
3. Glue or tape
4. Poster boards or large sheets of paper
5. Markers, colored pencils, or crayons
6. Personal notebooks or journals

Thoughts

become

Things

Instructions:

1. Introduction (15 minutes):
- Begin the exercise by discussing the importance of long-term thinking and its role in the journey to college. Emphasize the significance of setting clear goals aligned with individual passions and aspirations.

2. Goal Setting (15 minutes):
- Guide students in reflecting on their long-term goals for college and beyond. Ask them to write down specific goals related to academics, extracurricular activities, personal development, and career aspirations in their notebooks.

3. Vision Board Explanation (10 minutes):
- Explain the concept of a vision board and how it serves as a powerful tool for visualizing and manifesting goals. Describe how each element on the board should represent a specific aspect of their long-term vision.

4. Collage Creation (45 minutes):
- Provide magazines, newspapers, or printed images that students can use to create their vision boards. Instruct them to cut out images, words, and phrases that resonate with their goals and aspirations. Encourage creativity and the inclusion of diverse elements.

5. Board Assembly (15 minutes):
- Distribute poster boards or large sheets of paper, glue or tape, and markers. Instruct students to arrange and affix their chosen images and words onto their boards, creating a visually appealing representation of their long-term goals.

6. Reflection (15 minutes):
- After completing their vision boards, ask students to reflect on the process. In their notebooks, have them answer the following questions:

- What specific elements on your vision board represent your academic goals?
- How did the exercise make you think about the importance of sustained efforts over time?
- What strategies can you implement to align your short-term actions with your long-term goals?

7. Presentation and Sharing (30 minutes):
- Allow students to share their vision boards with the class. Each student can briefly discuss the elements on their board and the significance behind them. Encourage positive feedback and discussions about common themes among the boards.

8. Goal Commitment (15 minutes):
- Conclude the exercise by having students write a brief commitment statement in their notebooks. This statement should express their dedication to adopting a long-term mindset and taking strategic actions to navigate the path to college.

Homework/Extended Activity (Optional):
- Assign a follow-up essay or reflection where students articulate how their vision boards will guide their decision-making and actions over the coming months and years.

This exercise aims to translate the concept of long-term thinking into a tangible, visual representation of each student's aspirations. The vision board becomes a personal reminder of their journey's purpose, fostering motivation and determination to navigate the path to college with strategic intent.

Discussion Questions

1. Reflecting on Mr. Grant Money's journey in Pittsburgh, how do you think the city's vibrant energy and cultural richness might have influenced his perspective on long-term thinking and strategic planning for success?

2. Drawing parallels between Tony Dorsett's coast-to-coast run and the college journey, do you believe there are moments in education where adopting a long-term mindset is crucial, similar to the strategic planning and determination evident in a remarkable sports play? Share examples or personal experiences that support your viewpoint.

3. Considering the emphasis on sustained efforts for long-term success, how can students strike a balance between consistently investing time and energy into academic pursuits and maintaining a healthy work-life balance? What challenges might arise, and how can they be overcome?

4. In the story, Mr. Grant Money highlights the importance of aligning goals with passions and career aspirations for a long-term mindset. How can students explore and discover their passions early in their educational journey, and what role can schools and communities play in facilitating this alignment?

5. Reflecting on the concept of resilience and adaptability in the context of a long-term perspective, discuss instances in which setbacks or challenges can be viewed as opportunities for personal growth. How can educators and mentors help students develop resilience and see setbacks as valuable learning experiences rather than obstacles?

 Big Idea "The Resilience and Adaptability Curriculum"

Recognizing the importance of resilience and adaptability in the face of challenges, an innovative educational curriculum is proposed: The Resilience and Adaptability Curriculum. This curriculum would be integrated into high school and college programs, offering students practical tools and experiential learning opportunities to develop resilience skills. Workshops, real-world case studies, and mentorship programs would be incorporated to instill the mindset that setbacks are not roadblocks but stepping stones for personal growth. By embedding resilience education into the academic experience, students would be better equipped to navigate the inevitable challenges of their college journey and beyond.

🔍 Word Search

Discover these words hidden among the letters, each representing a facet of Mr. Grant Money's inspiring journey and the valuable lessons shared. Engage your mind and celebrate the fusion of Pittsburgh's allure with the wisdom of long-term thinking.

Immerse yourself in the bustling streets, iconic landmarks, and cherished memories as we explore the significance of long-term thinking versus short-term approaches in navigating the path to college. Happy word searching!

Now, here are the 14 words for the word search puzzle based on the story:

A	D	A	P	T	A	B	I	L	I	T	Y	T	L
E	N	R	E	S	I	L	I	E	N	C	E	E	D
E	W	A	I	N	R	O	F	I	L	A	C	I	T
T	O	S	P	P	I	T	T	S	B	U	R	G	H
I	D	D	T	S	I	E	N	T	I	O	T	T	E
S	H	T	E	I	H	T	T	R	E	N	Y	O	O
T	C	N	E	Y	P	I	L	T	O	N	Y	M	L
R	U	R	A	O	U	A	R	B	G	P	I	L	M
A	O	T	E	G	N	R	E	L	I	O	G	T	S
T	T	B	E	R	O	D	P	R	E	E	Y	N	A
E	T	M	U	I	N	T	T	I	C	Y	S	U	Y
G	H	O	N	T	T	S	T	E	E	L	Y	O	A
I	J	A	E	C	O	L	L	E	G	E	V	M	N
C	P	A	I	Y	T	I	S	R	E	V	I	N	U

TONY
JOURNAL
RESILIENCE
MOUNT
SHIRLEY
STEEL
PITTSBURGH
CALIFORNIA
ADAPTABILITY
TOUCHDOWN
STRIP
STRATEGIC
COLLEGE
UNIVERSITY

"Life's journey is a canvas painted with the strokes of our choices. The contrast between long-term thinking and short-term approaches is the difference between a carefully crafted masterpiece and a fleeting sketch."

SUCCESS STORIES

"Amidst Pittsburgh's innovation, a golden journal transformed me. Its wisdom, a beacon of long-term thinking"

In Pittsburgh, a city known for its rich history and innovation, Caroline, a student at the University of Pittsburgh, discovered a golden journal left on a bench on campus. This journal, filled with the wisdom and experiences of Mr. Grant Money, a figure renowned for his insights on success, became Caroline's unexpected source of inspiration. She was particularly moved by a story about Tony Dorsett's legendary football run, which epitomized the triumph of long-term thinking over short-term gains.

The contents of the journal prompted Caroline to reevaluate her approach to her academic and personal life. She realized that her focus on immediate results was limiting her potential. Inspired by the journal's teachings, Caroline began to align her goals with her passions, particularly in technology and community service. She started investing more in her research projects and engaged actively in community outreach, building a network of mentors and peers.

Caroline's new approach led to a significant transformation. Her consistent efforts in various projects and her engagement in the community reflected her understanding of the importance of each step in her long-term journey. Despite facing challenges and moments of doubt, Caroline's resilience and adaptability, fostered by the lessons from the journal, helped her turn obstacles into opportunities for growth.

As Caroline concluded her undergraduate studies, she emerged not just as an academically accomplished student but also as a leader and an inspiration to others. Her journey was marked by a blend of academic excellence and personal development, fueled by her long-term vision and the wisdom gleaned from the journal.

Years later, as a successful professional, Caroline often reflected on the impact of the golden journal and its role as a catalyst in her journey. Her story became synonymous with the power of long-term thinking and strategic planning, mirroring the essence of Pittsburgh's transformation from a steel-centric past to a hub of modern innovation. Caroline's success story is a testament to the enduring value of aligning one's efforts with a broader, long-term vision.

Sustaining Success: A Golden Serenade

Mr. Grant Money's Encore Lesson On Perseverance, Adaptability, And The Unseen Symphony Of Achieving Goals

On a crisp winter day in Cleveland, Ohio, Mr. Grant Money found himself bundled up in a stylish overcoat, eagerly attending a musical recital at the magnificent Severance Hall. The grandeur of the venue and the anticipation of the performance filled the air with an air of sophistication and cultural richness.

As Mr. Grant Money settled into his seat, he marveled at the architecture of Severance Hall. The name itself triggered a train of thought, connecting with the word "perseverance." The very essence of the hall seemed to embody the spirit of perseverance—a quality that resonated deeply with Mr. Grant Money as he reflected on his adventurous journeys and the invaluable lessons he had learned along the way.

The lights dimmed, and the soothing melodies began to fill the hall. The music, like a gentle breeze, wrapped around the audience, transporting them into a world of harmony. Mr. Grant Money, nearly lulled into a peaceful slumber by the relaxing sounds, was suddenly jolted awake by an unusual interruption.

A hushed murmur rippled through the audience as the sustain pedal of the grand piano got stuck, creating an awkward and sustained sound that lingered for what felt like an eternity, though it lasted only a few seconds. The pianist gracefully navigated through the unexpected glitch, seamlessly incorporating it into the performance.

Amidst the unexpected discord, Mr. Grant Money made a mental note. This moment, he thought, encapsulated a profound lesson about success—it requires sustained effort, much like the pedal that got stuck. The ability to persevere through challenges and maintain momentum in the face of unexpected hiccups is a key ingredient in the recipe for achieving one's goals.

The next day, Mr. Grant Money found himself at a local high school in Cleveland, ready to share this insightful lesson with the students. As he stood in front of the eager audience, he spoke passionately about the concept of sustained effort and what it truly looks like on the journey to success.

Five Points about Sustained Effort: Navigating the Path to Success

1. Consistency Over Time
- Sustained effort involves consistent action over an extended period. Success is not achieved through sporadic bursts of activity but through a commitment to daily, weekly, and monthly progress.

2. Resilience in the Face of Challenges
- Challenges and setbacks are inevitable, much like the stuck sustain pedal in the piano performance. Sustained effort requires resilience—the ability to bounce back, adapt, and persevere through difficulties.

3. Adaptability and Adjustments
- Successful individuals understand the need for adaptability. Just as the pianist adjusted to the unexpected glitch, those on the path to success must be willing to reassess, adapt, and make necessary adjustments to their strategies.

4. Maintaining Focus on Long-Term Goals
- Sustained effort is purposeful and focused on long-term goals. It involves keeping a clear vision of the destination while navigating the day-to-day challenges that may arise.

5. Continuous Learning and Growth

- The journey to success is a learning process. Sustained effort includes a commitment to continuous learning, growth, and improvement. It's about refining skills, acquiring new knowledge, and evolving along the way.

As Mr. Grant Money concluded his talk, he left the students with a powerful message: "Success is not a sprint; it's a sustained effort, much like the piano pedal that got stuck. Embrace challenges, stay focused on your goals, and persevere. The symphony of success is played with determination and resilience."

With that, he made a final note in his Golden Journal, a record of yet another lesson learned in the pursuit of knowledge and the sharing of wisdom. As he clutched his Shirley Scepter, Mr. Grant Money looked forward to the next chapter of his adventurous journey, knowing that the echoes of sustained effort would resonate with those who had listened.

"In the grand symphony of success, sustained effort is the melody that carries us through unexpected glitches. Just like a stuck piano pedal, challenges are moments to persevere, not reasons to falter. Embrace the discord, adjust your notes, and play on with determination."

- Mr. Grant Money

Exercise: "Symphony of Sustained Effort Reflection"

Objective: This exercise aims to deepen students' understanding of sustained effort and its role in achieving success. Through personal reflection and group discussion, students will explore the concept of perseverance and develop strategies to integrate sustained effort into their academic and personal journeys.

Materials Needed:
1. Notebooks or paper
2. Writing implements
3. Whiteboard and markers (for group discussion if applicable)

Instructions:

1. Introduction (15 minutes):
- Begin the exercise by recapping Mr. Grant Money's story about the piano sustain pedal and its connection to sustained effort. Emphasize the importance of consistency, resilience, and adaptability in navigating the path to success.

2. Personal Reflection (20 minutes):
- Ask students to take some time to reflect on the following questions in their notebooks:

- Can you think of a time in your life when you faced a challenge or setback?
- How did you respond to that challenge, and what did you learn from the experience?
- In what areas of your life do you feel you need to apply more sustained effort?

3. Group Discussion (20 minutes):
- If the class allows, organize students into small groups. On a whiteboard, prompt the following discussion questions:

- Share a personal experience related to sustained effort and overcoming challenges.
- Discuss how sustained effort can contribute to academic success.
- Brainstorm strategies for maintaining focus on long-term goals.

Encourage open discussions and the sharing of insights among group members.

4. Goal Setting (15 minutes):
- In their notebooks, have students set one short-term and one long-term goal. Emphasize that these goals should align with their aspirations and require sustained effort for achievement.

5. Action Plan (20 minutes):
- Ask students to develop a practical action plan for achieving their goals. This plan should include specific, achievable steps, a timeline, and potential challenges they may encounter.

6. Presentation (15 minutes):
- Provide an opportunity for students to share their goals and action plans with the class. This could be through verbal presentations, written summaries, or creative expressions such as drawings or diagrams.

7. Reflection and Commitment (15 minutes):
- Conclude the exercise with a final reflection. Have students answer the following questions in their notebooks:

- How does the concept of sustained effort resonate with you personally?
- What insights have you gained from the exercise, and how will you apply them to your journey?

Homework/Extended Activity (Optional):
- Assign a follow-up assignment where students track their progress toward their goals over the next few weeks and reflect on the impact of sustained effort on their journey.

This exercise encourages students to internalize the concept of sustained effort and apply it to their individual goals. By combining personal reflection, group discussion, goal setting, and action planning, students gain a comprehensive understanding of perseverance as a key element in achieving success.

"As I sat in Severance Hall, surrounded by the echoes of perseverance, I realized: Success is not a one-time performance but a daily commitment. Like the pianist who turned a glitch into harmony, we must navigate challenges with resilience. Sustained effort is the key to unlocking the full score of achievement."

- Mr. Grant Money

Discussion Questions

1. How does the unexpected glitch in the piano performance symbolize the importance of resilience in the journey to success, and can you think of a personal experience where you had to navigate through a challenge to achieve your goals?

2. In what ways does the stuck sustain pedal serve as a metaphor for the challenges we encounter in life, and how can individuals learn to gracefully incorporate unexpected disruptions into their paths towards success?

3. Mr. Grant Money emphasizes both consistency and adaptability on the road to success. How do you strike a balance between maintaining a consistent effort towards your goals and being flexible enough to adapt to unforeseen circumstances or changes in your plans?

4. According to Mr. Grant Money, sustained effort involves a commitment to continuous learning and growth. Can you share an example from your own life where acquiring new knowledge or skills played a crucial role in overcoming obstacles and achieving success?

5. Discuss the idea of maintaining focus on long-term goals while navigating day-to-day challenges. How do you personally ensure that you stay committed to your overarching objectives even when faced with immediate difficulties or distractions?

💡 Big Idea "Perseverance Pillars Architectural Project"

Inspired by the connection Mr. Grant Money made between Severance Hall and the word "perseverance," initiate an architectural project named "Perseverance Pillars." Collaborate with local artists, architects, and city officials to identify prominent public spaces where symbolic pillars can be constructed. Each pillar will represent one of the five points about sustained effort, visually showcasing the concepts of consistency, resilience, adaptability, focus on long-term goals, and continuous learning. The project not only serves as a visual reminder of the lessons shared by Mr. Grant Money but also promotes a sense of community engagement and a shared commitment to perseverance.

🔍 Word Search

Embark on a captivating word search puzzle inspired by the remarkable journey of Mr. Grant Money, a seasoned adventurer with a penchant for sharing invaluable lessons. Join him as he experiences the grandeur of Severance Hall, reflects on the essence of perseverance, and imparts a powerful message about sustained effort.

As you delve into this word search, discover the words that encapsulate the spirit of Mr. Grant Money's tale and the five key points he shared about navigating the path to success.

Now, here are the 15 words for the word search puzzle based on the story:

C	O	N	S	I	S	T	E	N	C	Y	E	Y	S
A	E	P	S	H	T	R	O	F	F	E	J	E	E
S	S	S	E	C	C	U	S	A	E	T	O	M	T
T	F	E	M	H	G	A	T	D	C	A	U	Y	L
N	O	G	E	A	N	E	E	A	N	H	R	S	A
E	C	O	N	L	I	E	C	P	A	S	N	I	D
M	U	A	N	L	N	C	N	T	R	Y	E	Y	V
T	S	L	C	E	R	U	E	A	E	M	Y	G	E
S	T	S	O	N	A	E	I	B	V	P	W	R	N
U	V	E	S	G	E	E	L	I	E	H	A	O	T
J	N	U	E	E	L	C	I	L	S	O	A	W	U
D	N	G	R	S	T	A	S	I	R	N	M	T	R
A	D	O	A	N	E	P	E	T	E	Y	S	H	E
S	O	P	Y	S	V	A	R	Y	P	R	E	I	C

CONSISTENCY
PERSEVERANCE
RESILIENCE
GROWTH
CHALLENGES
ADVENTURE
GOALS
JOURNEY
FOCUS
EFFORT
SYMPHONY
ADAPTABILITY
ADJUSTMENTS
LEARNING
SUCCESS

"Life's melody is composed of sustained efforts, a harmonious blend of consistency, resilience, adaptability, focus, and continuous growth. Just as a pianist navigates a stuck sustain pedal, our journey to success is marked by the ability to turn challenges into opportunities and maintain unwavering determination."

SUCCESS STORIES

"Brushstrokes of Resilience: Mikaela's Journey from Business to Canvas, Defying Expectations and Redefining Success"

Mikaela, a budding artist from New York City, was initially drawn to the world of art but succumbed to societal pressures and chose a practical business degree during her college years. However, her passion for art persisted, and a discovery of her grandmother's old journal rekindled her artistic dreams. This turning point led her to change her major to fine arts, a decision that challenged her family's expectations and brought uncertainty to her future.

Despite her determination, Mikaela faced numerous obstacles on her journey to becoming a successful artist. The art world can be competitive and unforgiving, and she encountered rejection and setbacks along the way. Her path was marked by financial instability as she pursued her passion, a stark contrast to the stability she would have had in a business career. These hurdles tested her resolve and forced her to confront the societal notion of success tied to financial security.

Mikaela's story underscores her perseverance and resilience. She continued to nurture her artistic talent, experimenting with various styles and techniques while participating in small gallery exhibitions and local art shows. Through these experiences, she slowly but steadily gained recognition for her unique style, which incorporated elements of city life and nature's beauty.

As the years passed, Mikaela's art career flourished. Her work gained recognition in prominent art publications, and collectors from around the world sought her paintings. She transformed her grandmother's journal into a testament to her journey of self-discovery and the courage to follow her passion. Mikaela's story serves as a powerful reminder that success is not solely measured by financial gain but also by the pursuit of one's deepest passions and the fulfillment of lifelong dreams, despite the obstacles faced along the way.

Sunset Wisdom: Mr. Grant Money's Guide to Acing ACT and SAT

In the enchanting backdrop of Key West, Mr. Grant Money crafts an illuminating plan to help Wichita students navigate the challenges of standardized tests, ensuring a bright future.

Under the warm Florida sun, Mr. Grant Money found himself embarking on an exciting adventure in Key West. The vibrant colors of the bougainvillea, the lively music drifting from the streets, and the scent of saltwater in the air created an atmosphere of pure joy. Every moment in Key West was a treasure, from exploring the historic Old Town to witnessing the breathtaking sunset at Mallory Square.

After days of immersing himself in the local culture and traversing the main attractions, Mr. Grant Money returned to his luxury suite, where a letter from Valencia, a dedicated member of the Power House Crew, awaited him. The letter conveyed the earnest request from a group of Wichita, Kansas, students seeking guidance on preparing for the ACT and SAT exams.

Seated at his laptop, surrounded by the echoes of Key West adventures, Mr. Grant Money smiled, acknowledging the importance of the student's inquiry. He began crafting a detailed response, outlining a comprehensive 8-point game plan to help them navigate the challenges of standardized testing and prepare for success.

Mr. Grant Money's 8-Point Game Plan for ACT and SAT Success:

1. Early Assessment
- Start by taking a practice test for the ACT and SAT to identify strengths and areas needing improvement. Early assessment provides a baseline for your preparation journey.

2. Strategic Focus
- Identify the sections where you need the most improvement. Allocate more study time to these areas, but don't neglect the sections where you excel. Balancing strengths and weaknesses is key.

3. Consistent Study Schedule
- Establish a consistent study schedule that aligns with your daily routine. Consistency is crucial for building a strong foundation of knowledge and developing effective test-taking strategies.

4. Resource Utilization
- Explore a variety of study resources, including practice tests, review books, and online materials. Utilize reputable platforms and take advantage of available tools to enhance your understanding of the exam content.

5. Effective Time Management
- Practice time management strategies while taking practice tests. Simulate test conditions to improve pacing and ensure you can complete each section within the allotted time.

6. Review and Adapt
- Regularly review your progress and adapt your study plan accordingly. If certain strategies or study methods aren't yielding results, be flexible and explore alternative approaches.

7. Mock Exams
- Schedule regular mock exams to simulate real testing conditions. This helps build endurance and familiarizes you with the test environment, reducing anxiety on exam day.

8. Healthy Lifestyle
- Prioritize a healthy lifestyle, including proper sleep, nutrition, and exercise. A well-balanced lifestyle positively impacts cognitive function and overall well-being, contributing to better test performance.

As Mr. Grant Money finished typing the last point, he couldn't help but reflect on the impact such guidance could have had on his own educational journey. A sense of gratitude washed over him as he chuckled at the thought of the possibilities if he had possessed this knowledge and discipline in his youth.

With a smile on his face, Mr. Grant Money sealed the letter, confident that his insights would empower the students in Wichita to approach the ACT and SAT with a strategic mindset. As he pressed send, he felt a renewed sense of purpose, knowing that his adventures not only enriched his own life but also allowed him to share valuable lessons with the next generation.

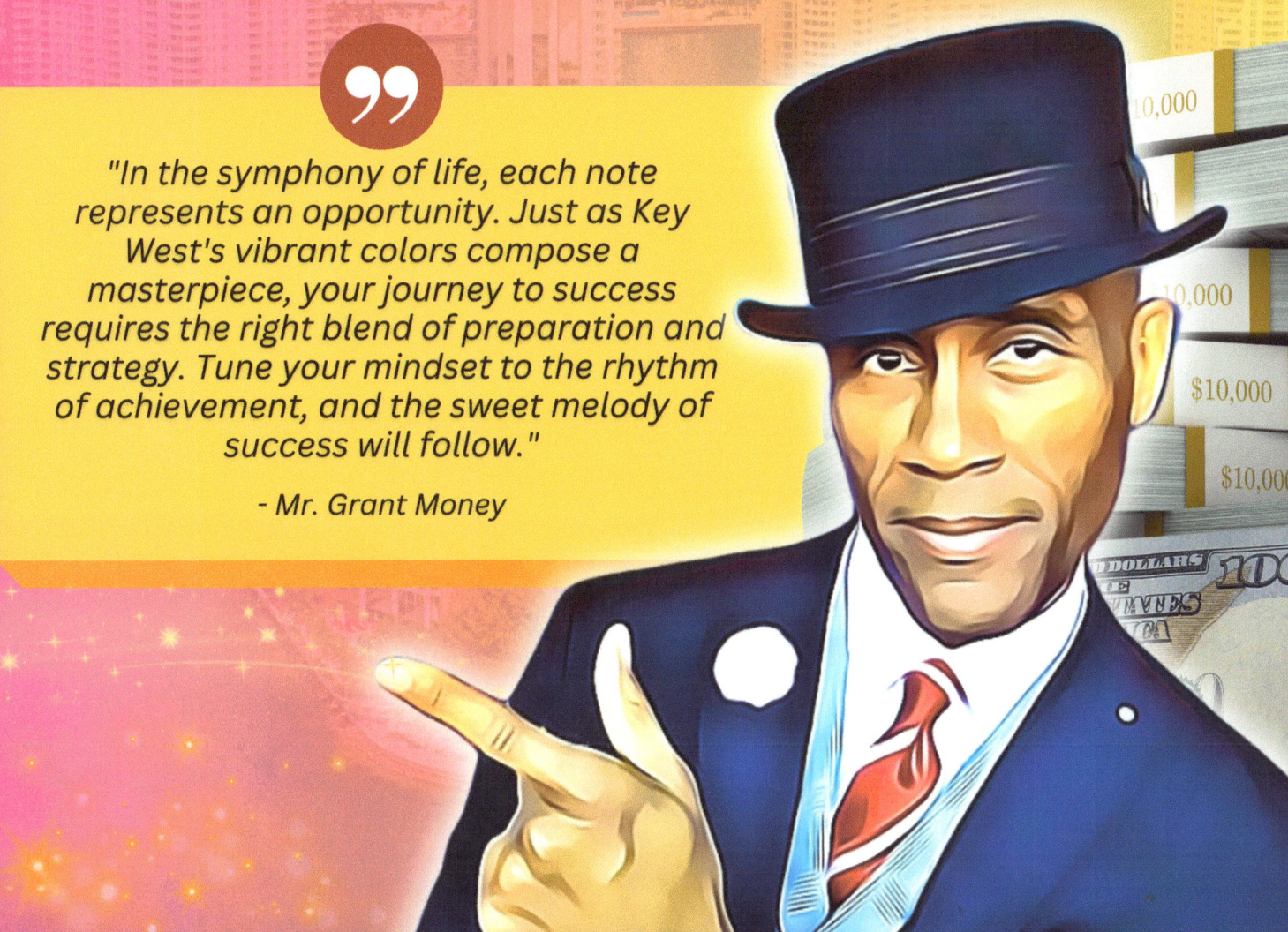

"In the symphony of life, each note represents an opportunity. Just as Key West's vibrant colors compose a masterpiece, your journey to success requires the right blend of preparation and strategy. Tune your mindset to the rhythm of achievement, and the sweet melody of success will follow."

- Mr. Grant Money

Exercise: "ACT and SAT Success Action Plan"

Objective: This exercise aims to engage students in a practical and comprehensive approach to preparing for the ACT and SAT exams. Students will gain insights into effective study strategies and test-taking techniques by breaking down the preparation process into actionable steps.

Materials Needed:
1. Whiteboard and markers (or chart paper and markers)
2. Access to online study resources
3. Notebooks or paper for students

Instructions:

1. Introduction (10 minutes):
- Begin the exercise by discussing the importance of preparing strategically for standardized tests like the ACT and SAT. Emphasize that effective preparation involves a combination of knowledge, skills, and mindset.

2. Recap Mr. Grant Money's Game Plan (15 minutes):
- Recap Mr. Grant Money's 8-point game plan for ACT and SAT success. Discuss each point briefly, highlighting the significance of early assessment, strategic focus, consistent study schedules, and other key elements.

3. Group Brainstorming (20 minutes):
- Divide the class into small groups and provide each group with a whiteboard or chart paper. Instruct them to brainstorm additional strategies or tips that could complement Mr. Grant Money's game plan. Encourage creativity and collaboration.

4. Group Presentation (20 minutes):
- Each group presents their additional strategies to the class. Discuss the merits of each suggestion and how it contributes to a well-rounded ACT and SAT preparation plan.

5. Personal Reflection (15 minutes):
- Individually, ask students to reflect on the group presentations and select three strategies that resonate with them. In their notebooks, have them explain why they find these strategies valuable and how they plan to incorporate them into their study routine.

6. Online Resource Exploration (20 minutes):

- Guide students to explore reputable online resources for ACT and SAT preparation. This could include practice tests, study guides, and interactive tools. Discuss the importance of utilizing diverse resources to comprehensively understand the exam content.

7. Mock Exam Simulation (30 minutes):

- Conduct a mock exam simulation in the classroom. Provide practice test booklets or online resources, and mimic test conditions as closely as possible. Afterward, discuss the experience and strategies for improving time management and performance.

8. Group Action Plan (20 minutes):

- In their groups, students create an action plan that incorporates both Mr. Grant Money's game plan and the additional strategies brainstormed earlier. The plan should outline specific tasks, deadlines, and individual responsibilities.

9. Goal Setting and Commitment (15 minutes):

- Have each student set specific goals for their ACT and SAT preparation. Encourage them to articulate these goals in their notebooks and make a commitment to following through with their action plans.

10. Closing Reflection (10 minutes):

- Conclude the exercise with a brief class discussion. Ask students to share one insight they gained from the exercise and how they feel more prepared for their ACT and SAT exams. Emphasize the importance of sustained effort and strategic thinking in achieving success.

This exercise provides students with actionable steps for ACT and SAT preparation and encourages collaboration, reflection, and goal-setting. By incorporating both Mr. Grant Money's insights and student-generated strategies, the exercise aims to create a holistic and personalized approach to standardized test preparation.

"Life's adventure, much like exploring the charming streets of Old Town, is a series of tests. The key is not merely to survive but to thrive. Approach each challenge with the precision of a well-crafted plan, and watch how your efforts transform into triumphs, much like the breathtaking sunset at Mallory Square."

- Mr. Grant Money

Discussion Questions

1. Mr. Grant Money reflects on the impact his guidance could have had on his own educational journey. How do you think access to such a comprehensive game plan for standardized testing might have influenced your own approach to exams during your school years?

2. Key West's vibrant culture and atmosphere play a significant role in the story. How do you think cultural experiences, like those in Key West, can contribute to a person's mindset and effectiveness in addressing academic challenges or providing guidance to others?

3. Mr. Grant Money emphasizes the importance of strategic focus and balancing strengths and weaknesses in test preparation. Can you share a personal experience where identifying and focusing on specific areas for improvement positively impacted your academic or professional performance?

4. The game plan suggests regularly reviewing progress and being adaptable in study methods. In your opinion, how crucial is the ability to adapt in the learning process, and can you share an example from your own education where flexibility in study approaches led to improved outcomes?

5. Mr. Grant Money's experiences in Key West lead to him sharing valuable insights with students in Wichita. How can personal experiences, whether adventurous or challenging, shape one's ability to provide meaningful guidance and support to others, especially in educational contexts?

💡 Big Idea "Standardized Test Success Platform"

Building off Mr. Grant Money's 8-point game plan, there's an opportunity to create a comprehensive online platform dedicated to standardized test success. This platform could provide personalized study plans based on initial assessments, interactive study materials, simulated testing environments, and progress tracking. By incorporating adaptive learning technology and data analytics, the platform could continuously refine its recommendations, ensuring that students receive targeted support where they need it most. This tool would not only be useful for students in Wichita but could cater to a broader audience, addressing the universal challenge of preparing for standardized tests.

🔍 Word Search

Immerse yourself in the vibrant world of Mr. Grant Money's journey through the enchanting streets of Key West, Florida. As he basked in the warm sunshine and reveled in the cultural delights of this tropical paradise, Mr. Grant Money received a heartfelt letter from Valencia of the Power House Crew.

Unearth these words in the puzzle to reveal the essence of Mr. Grant Money's wisdom. Happy word searching, and may your journey be as enriching as his adventures in Key West!

Now, here are the 15 words for the word search puzzle based on the story:

E	W	E	I	V	E	R	L	T	U	S	C	W	T
A	S	S	E	S	S	M	E	N	T	E	O	E	M
C	R	S	T	N	E	M	E	G	A	N	A	M	N
I	A	A	C	A	E	H	T	L	A	H	A	X	I
G	T	A	O	L	V	E	M	E	U	L	S	L	X
E	N	R	N	I	A	A	O	H	A	X	Y	N	E
T	T	E	S	F	L	L	C	S	E	M	U	Y	A
A	E	S	I	E	E	T	K	U	E	X	N	R	A
R	C	O	S	S	N	H	W	I	C	E	E	Y	Y
T	E	U	T	T	C	Y	R	T	E	A	E	E	E
S	E	R	E	Y	I	O	E	E	V	M	S	T	I
S	A	C	N	L	A	G	S	A	I	E	A	T	S
P	U	E	T	E	E	T	E	T	S	M	A	X	E
T	P	A	D	A	A	N	M	R	E	E	N	U	G

VALENCIA
LUXURY
MANAGEMENT
EXAMS
ADAPT
LIFESTYLE
HEALTHY
RESOURCE
TIME
SUITE
ASSESSMENT
CONSISTENT
STRATEGIC
MOCK
REVIEW

"Amidst the lively music and saltwater breeze, Mr. Grant Money penned a letter, weaving guidance as intricate as the bougainvillea's blooms. The wisdom shared with Wichita students is a testament to the belief that education, like a treasured adventure, has the power to unlock doors and illuminate paths to success."

SUCCESS STORIES

"Empowering Dreams: Elou's Journey to Academic Success and Holistic Development with Mr. Grant Money's Guidance"

Elou, a dedicated educator from Wichita, Kansas, had always been passionate about helping her students achieve their academic dreams. However, she faced a unique challenge when a group of her students expressed their desire to excel in the ACT and SAT exams. The quest for guidance led her to reach out to Mr. Grant Money, a renowned expert known for his insightful advice.

As Elou eagerly awaited Mr. Grant Money's response, she couldn't help but reflect on her own journey as an educator. She had always been committed to her students' success, but the standardized testing landscape was evolving rapidly. She recognized the need to adapt her teaching methods to prepare her students adequately.

When Mr. Grant Money's detailed 8-point game plan arrived in her inbox, Elou felt a surge of optimism. The comprehensive advice provided a roadmap for her students' success. She meticulously crafted a plan to incorporate Mr. Grant Money's recommendations into her teaching, emphasizing the importance of early assessment and strategic focus.

Over time, Elou witnessed a remarkable transformation in her students. They embraced the consistent study schedule, diligently practiced time management strategies, and incorporated healthy lifestyle habits into their routines. As they took regular mock exams, their confidence grew, and their performance improved.

Elou's dedication to her students and her willingness to adapt her teaching methods to align with Mr. Grant Money's guidance bore fruit. Her students not only excelled in the ACT and SAT exams but also developed essential life skills, such as discipline, time management, and resilience.

Personally, Elou felt a sense of fulfillment that transcended the classroom. She had evolved as an educator, embracing innovative strategies and nurturing her students' holistic development. Her journey with Mr. Grant Money's guidance had not only enhanced her professional skills but also deepened her commitment to helping students unlock their full potential.

As she looked back on the journey, Elou realized that her role as an educator extended far beyond imparting knowledge; it was about empowering students to navigate challenges, set ambitious goals, and achieve success. With a renewed sense of purpose, she continued to inspire and guide her students, knowing that the impact of her dedication reached far beyond standardized tests, leaving an indelible mark on their lives.

Ink and Ivory Dreams: Mr. Grant Money's Midnight Mission to Rewrite a College Essay

When Dreams Collide with Reality—A Journey Through the Labyrinth of Personal Narratives, Achievements, and the Symphony of Structure

Mr. Grant Money, the epitome of sartorial elegance, boarded the first-class cabin of his flight to Washington with an air of sophistication. His three-piece suit, adorned with a perfectly tied bow tie, a white shirt, and a hat that added a touch of flair, commanded attention. Customized cufflinks embroidered with the initials MGM on his cuffs spoke of his attention to detail and unique style. As he settled into his seat, the stewardess couldn't help but compliment his impeccable attire and the subtle, delightful fragrance that lingered around him.

With a gracious smile, Mr. Grant Money acknowledged the compliment and settled into his plush first-class seat. The hum of the airplane's engines and the gentle rocking lulled him into a peaceful slumber. Little did he know that his journey would take an unexpected turn into the realm of dreams.

In the vivid landscape of his dream, Mr. Grant Money found himself in a surreal world where an elephant, Jerla, communicated in a language known only to elephants. The majestic creature spoke urgently, flapping its ears and trumpeting, trying to convey a critical message. The message, deciphered through an otherworldly connection, indicated a counterclockwise error that needed attention.

As the dream unfolded, Mr. Grant Money realized that Jerla, his angelic guide, was sending a profound message related to his mission to help students. The counterclockwise turn symbolized a misdirection in the path of a student named Lisa. In the dream, Lisa was constructing her college essay incorrectly, and Jerla implored Mr. Grant Money to intervene and guide her on the right path.

Three Mistakes Lisa Was Making in Her College Essay:

1. Lack of Personal Voice
- Lisa's essay lacked her unique voice and perspective. It read more like a generic piece than a personal narrative, failing to convey her individuality and experiences.

2. Weak Structure and Organization
- The essay lacked a clear and compelling structure. Ideas were scattered, making it difficult for the reader to follow a coherent narrative. A strong essay should have a clear introduction, body, and conclusion.

3. Overemphasis on Achievements
- Lisa's essay overly focused on achievements and accolades, failing to delve into the personal growth, challenges faced, and lessons learned. A compelling college essay goes beyond the surface and reveals the applicant's character and resilience.

Jerla's communication in the dream revealed Mr. Grant Money's crucial role, He was to appear to Lisa in a dream, gently guiding her toward a more effective approach to her college essay.

Five Important Points for Crafting an Exceptional College Essay:

1. Authenticity
- Emphasize authenticity. Share personal stories, experiences, and perspectives that genuinely reflect who you are. Let your voice shine through.

2. Compelling Introduction
- Craft a captivating introduction that hooks the reader and sets the tone for the entire essay. A strong opening creates intrigue and captures attention.

3. Structured Narrative
- Organize your essay with a clear structure. Ensure a logical flow from introduction to body to conclusion, allowing the reader to follow your narrative effortlessly.

4. Personal Growth and Reflection
- Share not only your achievements but also moments of personal growth, challenges overcome, and reflections on your journey. This depth adds layers to your character.

5. Impactful Conclusion
- Conclude your essay with a powerful statement that leaves a lasting impression. A well-crafted conclusion ties together the themes and emotions expressed throughout the essay.

As Mr. Grant Money shared these insights in the dream, he felt a profound connection to his mission. The dream abruptly ended when the airline stewardess touched him gently, signaling the plane's arrival in Washington.

Deboarding the plane, Mr. Grant Money took a moment to gather his thoughts. The dream lingered in his mind, leaving him in awe of the guidance he had received. He opened his golden journal, the repository of wisdom, and penned a powerful quote:

"In the tapestry of college essays, the threads of authenticity, structure, and reflection weave a masterpiece that echoes the individuality of the storyteller."

With a smile of gratitude, Mr. Grant Money looked forward to the journey ahead, knowing that he held the keys to unlock the potential of students like Lisa, guiding them toward creating essays that not only impress but also resonate on a deeply personal level.

"Just as a finely tailored suit speaks volumes about a person, a college essay should be crafted with the same precision—woven with threads of authenticity, structured elegance, and the reflective essence that makes each applicant's story a masterpiece."

- Mr. Grant Money

Exercise: "Crafting Your Exceptional College Essay"

Objective: This exercise aims to guide students in applying the insights from Mr. Grant Money's dream to create a compelling and authentic college essay. Through a step-by-step process, students will focus on developing their unique voice, structuring their narrative, and incorporating personal growth and reflection.

Materials Needed:
1. Notebooks or paper
2. Writing implements
3. Access to online resources (optional)

Instructions:

1. Introduction to Exceptional College Essays (15 minutes):
- Begin the exercise by discussing the importance of a compelling college essay and its role in the admissions process. Introduce the key elements highlighted by Mr. Grant Money's dream: authenticity, structured narrative, and personal growth.

2. Reflect on Personal Experiences (20 minutes):
- Ask students to reflect on significant personal experiences, challenges overcome, or moments of growth. Encourage them to jot down key events, emotions, and reflections related to their journey.

3. Crafting a Captivating Introduction (20 minutes):
- Guide students in crafting a captivating introduction for their essays. Discuss strategies such as starting with a personal anecdote, posing a thought-provoking question, or sharing a unique perspective. Emphasize the importance of hooking the reader from the beginning.

4. Structuring the Narrative (30 minutes):
- Discuss the importance of a clear structure in a college essay. Help students outline their essays with a logical flow, including introduction, body, and conclusion. Share examples of effective transitions between paragraphs.

5. Incorporating Personal Growth and Reflection (25 minutes):
- Encourage students to delve into moments of personal growth, challenges faced, and lessons learned. Discuss the significance of going beyond achievements and showcasing self-awareness and resilience.

6. Peer Review (20 minutes):
- Organize a peer review session where students exchange drafts of their essays. Provide a checklist for peers to assess elements like authenticity, structure, and reflection. Encourage constructive feedback.

7. Revision and Feedback (20 minutes):
- Based on peer feedback, give students time to revise their essays. Offer individualized feedback, focusing on areas of improvement and highlighting the strengths of their narratives.

8. Final Reflection (15 minutes):
- Conclude the exercise with a final reflection. Ask students to reflect on the process of crafting their college essays, what they learned about themselves in the process, and how they incorporated the principles highlighted by Mr. Grant Money.

Homework/Extended Activity (Optional):
- Assign a reflective essay where students articulate the significance of their chosen personal experiences and the impact of the writing process on their understanding of themselves.

This exercise provides students with a practical approach to applying the insights from Mr. Grant Money's dream. By guiding them through the steps of crafting an exceptional college essay, the exercise aims to empower students to express their unique voices and experiences in a way that resonates with admissions committees.

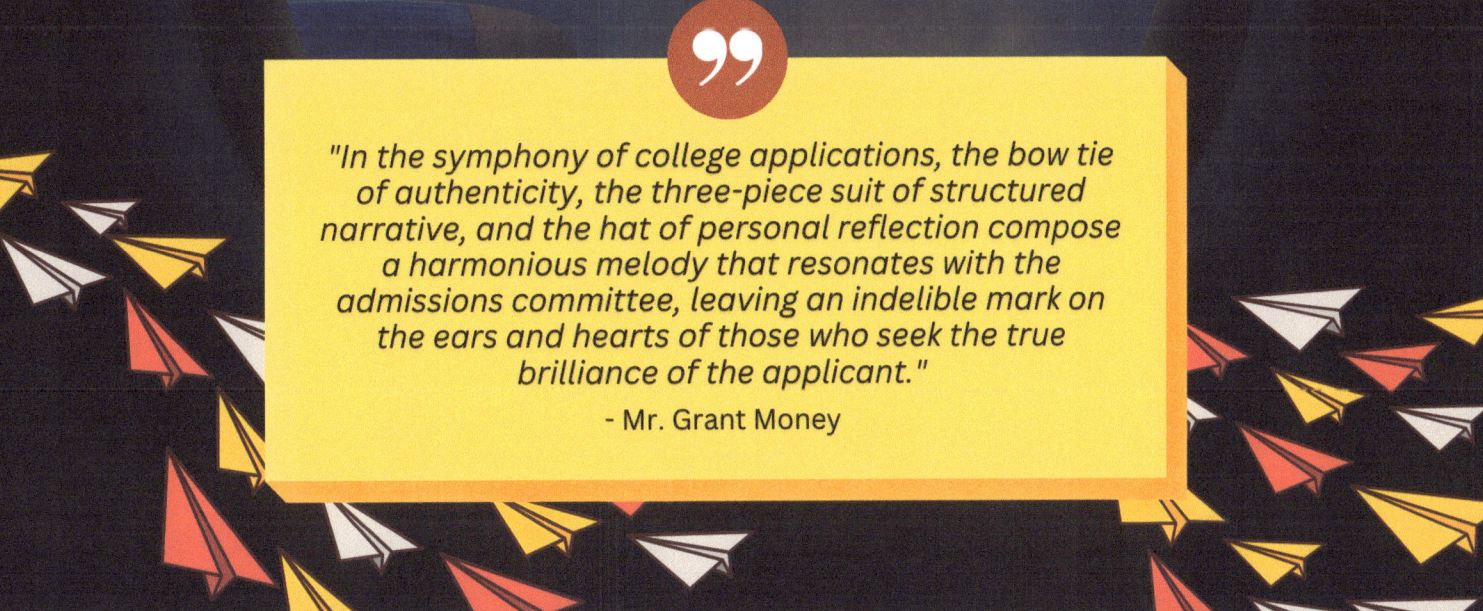

"In the symphony of college applications, the bow tie of authenticity, the three-piece suit of structured narrative, and the hat of personal reflection compose a harmonious melody that resonates with the admissions committee, leaving an indelible mark on the ears and hearts of those who seek the true brilliance of the applicant."

- Mr. Grant Money

Discussion Questions

1. Dreams often carry symbolic messages. What could the counterclockwise turn symbolize in Mr. Grant Money's dream? How might the surreal elements, like an elephant communicating in an otherworldly language, relate to the challenges faced by students in their college essay writing journey?

2. Reflecting on Lisa's essay, why is it crucial for college essays to showcase the applicant's personal voice? How does a lack of personal voice impact the effectiveness of the essay in portraying the individuality of the applicant? Can you recall a personal experience where your unique voice played a pivotal role in expressing yourself?

3. Mr. Grant Money's dream served as a source of inspiration for guiding Lisa on her essay. Have you ever had a dream that provided clarity or inspiration in your waking life? How might dreams or subconscious thoughts influence creativity and problem-solving in various aspects of our lives?

4. The dream emphasized the importance of not overemphasizing achievements in a college essay. Why is it essential to strike a balance between showcasing achievements and delving into personal growth, challenges faced, and lessons learned? Can you think of a public figure or role model whose story effectively balances accomplishments and personal development?

5. How can Mr. Grant Money's dream and the insights gained be applied in the field of education and mentorship? In what ways can educators and mentors help students tap into their authentic voices and navigate the challenges of crafting compelling college essays? Can dream-like experiences serve as valuable teaching tools?

 ## Big Idea "College Essay Masterclass Series"

Mr. Grant Money decides to share his dream-guided wisdom on a broader scale through a College Essay Masterclass Series. Leveraging his experience and the insights gained from the dream, he creates a comprehensive online course. The series covers topics such as finding one's voice, crafting a compelling introduction, building a structured narrative, incorporating personal growth, and creating an impactful conclusion. The masterclass empowers students globally to elevate their college essay game, providing them with the tools and knowledge needed to stand out in the competitive college admissions process.

🔍 Word Search

Embark on a captivating word search adventure inspired by the remarkable journey of Mr. Grant Money, the embodiment of sartorial elegance and a beacon of wisdom. As he traversed the first-class skies to Washington, an unexpected dream unfolded, revealing insights that would shape the destiny of college-bound students.

Immerse yourself in the world of dreams, aspirations, and the art of crafting an exceptional college essay as you search the words intricately woven into the fabric of Mr. Grant Money's profound experience.

Now, here are the 14 words for the word search puzzle based on the story:

C	H	R	F	I	C	O	U	N	T	E	R	T	S
U	I	A	U	T	H	E	N	T	I	C	U	C	O
F	S	T	R	U	C	T	U	R	E	A	P	O	P
F	B	D	N	O	I	T	C	E	L	F	E	R	H
L	I	O	R	F	R	A	G	R	A	N	C	E	I
I	U	I	W	E	A	A	I	E	R	W	L	L	S
N	U	P	S	T	A	I	I	N	B	A	I	E	T
K	C	T	N	R	I	M	O	B	R	L	R	P	I
S	C	N	N	S	N	E	I	H	I	R	I	H	C
I	S	O	R	C	E	F	P	H	S	C	R	A	A
L	A	I	R	O	T	R	A	S	R	U	E	N	T
E	L	B	A	C	C	E	P	M	I	A	L	T	I
T	E	L	L	I	A	T	C	I	T	R	U	P	O
N	O	I	T	C	E	R	I	D	S	I	M	A	N

DREAM
BOWTIE
PLUSH
MISDIRECTION
STRUCTURE
ELEPHANT
COUNTER
REFLECTION
FRAGRANCE
SARTORIAL
AUTHENTIC
IMPECCABLE
SOPHISTICATION
CUFFLINKS

"In the realm of dreams, the guidance of an elephant may seem whimsical, but it's a metaphor for the unexpected sources of wisdom that can illuminate our paths. In the tapestry of life, whether crafting essays or navigating dreams, the threads of authenticity, structure, and introspection form a story that transcends the ordinary and becomes a work of art."

SUCCESS STORIES

"Threads of Triumph: Kathryn's Journey from Struggle to Success Through Authenticity, Structure, and Reflection"

In an article highlighting the transformative power of guidance and determination in the pursuit of academic dreams, Kathryn's success story stands out as an inspiring testament to resilience and mentorship. The backdrop is Washington, D.C., where Kathryn, a high school senior with dreams of attending a prestigious university, found herself facing a daunting challenge—crafting a compelling college essay. Despite her remarkable academic achievements and extracurricular involvement, she struggled to convey her unique voice and experiences effectively.

In her quest for guidance, Kathryn stumbled upon a golden journal inherited from her grandmother, containing a profound quote: "In the tapestry of life, it is the threads of authenticity, structure, and reflection that weave a masterpiece." Motivated by these words, she reached out to Mr. Grant Money, a renowned expert in college admissions, for assistance. Little did she know that this decision would set her on a remarkable journey of self-discovery and academic success.

A meeting with Mr. Grant Money in a quaint café marked the turning point in Kathryn's journey. With his signature sartorial elegance and compassionate demeanor, he listened to her struggles and fears attentively. Mr. Grant Money, drawing from insights received in a dream, emphasized the importance of authenticity, structure, and reflection in crafting a compelling college essay.

Empowered by this guidance, Kathryn embarked on a profound journey of self-reflection. She delved into her memories, embracing her personal growth, challenges overcome, and pivotal moments that had shaped her character. Her essay transformed into a masterpiece that not only showcased her achievements but also revealed her resilience, passion, and unique perspective. With a heart full of hope, she submitted her application to her dream university, awaiting the moment of validation.

Months later, the long-awaited acceptance letter arrived, filling Kathryn's heart with joy and pride. She had been admitted to her dream university, a testament to her unwavering determination and the transformative mentorship she had received from Mr. Grant Money. Her story, echoing far beyond her college acceptance, served as a reminder of the enduring value of authenticity, structure, and reflection in the pursuit of one's dreams.

In the years that followed, Kathryn thrived academically and personally, leaving an indelible mark on her university and the world. Her college essay had been the first thread in the tapestry of her success, symbolizing the power of resilience and mentorship in achieving one's aspirations. Kathryn's story illuminated the path for countless others, inspiring them to embrace their unique voices and pursue their dreams with unwavering determination.

MONUMENTS OF DESTINY

The Amazing Adventures of
MRGRANTMONEY

Monuments of Destiny: MGM's College Interview Chronicles

Embark on a unique adventure with Mr. Grant Money as he explores Washington, D.C., encounters an angelic guide

In the heart of Washington, D.C., Mr. Grant Money, or MGM as he was affectionately known, found himself in awe as he explored the key landmarks that symbolized the very essence of the nation's capital. The grandeur of the Capitol Building, the iconic White House, and the Pentagon left him speechless, and the larger-than-life statues of the Lincoln Monument and MLK's statue spoke to his soul in the most profound way.

MGM felt an overwhelming sense of encouragement as he marveled at these monumental structures. It was as if these historic landmarks were acknowledging and endorsing the meaningful work he was doing in helping students achieve their dreams. The statues stood as silent sentinels, guardians of the aspirations of generations past and future.

In the midst of his contemplation, a delicate butterfly gracefully landed on the right shoulder of his impeccably tailored suit. Turning to the right, he noticed a group of students heading toward the National Museum of African American History and Culture. Intuitively, MGM sensed that he was meant to go inside, even though the reason remained unclear.

Unbeknownst to him, Jerla, his angelic guide, had orchestrated this next chapter of his adventure. Inside the museum, amidst the profound stories of struggle, resilience, and triumph, MGM found himself in the company of a young high school student named Cedric from Baltimore. Their paths had converged for a purpose yet unknown.

The two struck up a conversation, and as Cedric shared his dreams of attending college, MGM soon discovered the reason for their serendipitous meeting. Cedric needed insight on preparing for his upcoming college interview, and MGM, with his wealth of experience, offered him sound advice.

MGM's 7-Point Advice on Preparing for a College Interview:

1. Self-Reflection
- Take time to reflect on your personal experiences, strengths, and areas of growth. Know yourself well, as this self-awareness will shine through during the interview.

2. Research the College
- Familiarize yourself with the college's values, mission, and culture. Understand why you are drawn to that particular institution and be prepared to articulate your genuine interest.

3. Practice Common Questions
- Anticipate and practice responses to common interview questions. This preparation will boost your confidence and ensure you communicate your thoughts effectively.

4. Highlight Achievements and Challenges
- Share your accomplishments, but also discuss challenges you've faced and how you've overcome them. Demonstrating resilience and growth adds depth to your story.

5. Ask Thoughtful Questions
- Prepare a few questions to ask the interviewer. This shows your genuine interest in the college and your proactive approach to your education.

6. Express Enthusiasm
- Let your passion and enthusiasm for your chosen field of study shine. Colleges look for students who are genuinely excited about their academic pursuits.

7. Follow Up
- Send a thank-you email to your interviewer expressing gratitude for the opportunity. Use this as a chance to reiterate your interest in the college and briefly mention any points you may have missed during the interview.

As the conversation unfolded, Cedric absorbed every word with enthusiasm. Grateful for the unexpected guidance, he left the museum with newfound confidence and excitement for his college journey.

Meanwhile, MGM continued to explore the exhibits, marveling at his ancestors' immense contributions to the country's development. The names Hoosie, PH, Fred Sr., Gracie, Emma, Minnie, Mabel, and many others crossed his mind.

With a smile on his face, he realized that he was continuing their legacy by empowering the youth of today. Inspired to do even more, MGM left the museum with a sense of purpose and a determination to be a beacon of guidance for the Cedrics of the world.

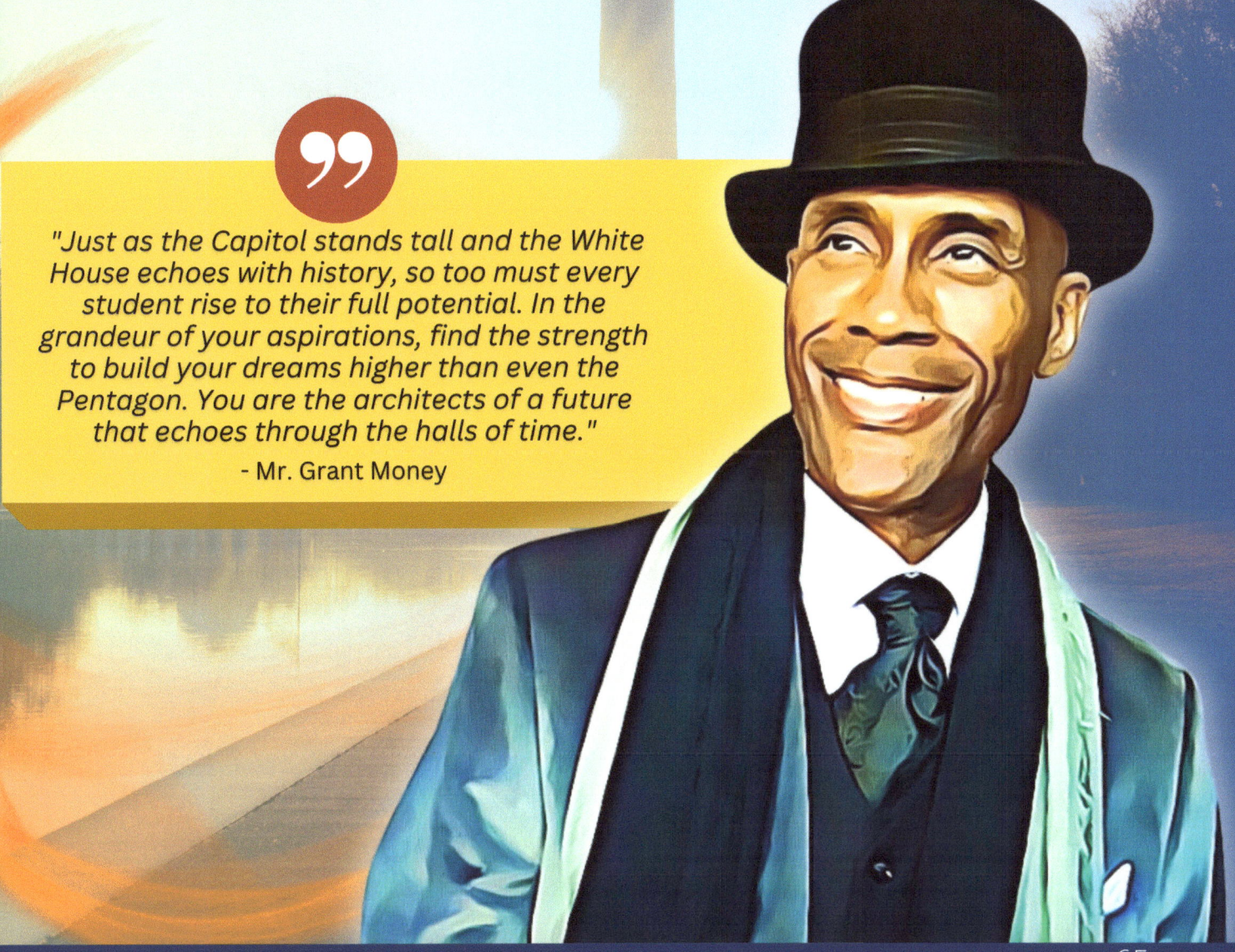

"Just as the Capitol stands tall and the White House echoes with history, so too must every student rise to their full potential. In the grandeur of your aspirations, find the strength to build your dreams higher than even the Pentagon. You are the architects of a future that echoes through the halls of time."
- Mr. Grant Money

Exercise: "College Interview Preparation"

Objective: This exercise aims to help students practice common college interview questions and prepare thoughtful questions to ask the interviewer. Students will enhance their interview skills and confidence by engaging in role-playing scenarios and thoughtful question formulation.

Materials Needed:
1. List of common college interview questions (provided below)
2. Whiteboard and markers (optional)
3. Notebooks or paper
4. Writing implements

Common College Interview Questions:
1. Tell me about yourself.
2. Why are you interested in our college?
3. What are your strengths and weaknesses?
4. Discuss a significant challenge you've faced and how you overcame it.
5. How do you envision contributing to campus life?
6. Describe a memorable academic experience.
7. What are your long-term goals and aspirations?
8. How do you handle stress or pressure?
9. Share an example of a time when you demonstrated leadership.
10. Is there anything else you would like to share that is not on your application?

Part 1: Practicing Common Interview Questions (40 minutes)

1. Introduction (5 minutes):
- Begin the exercise by discussing the importance of preparing for college interviews and their impact on the admissions process.

2. Explanation of Common Questions (10 minutes):
- Go through the list of common college interview questions with the students. Discuss each question briefly, providing insights into what interviewers seek in the responses.

3. Role-Playing Scenarios (25 minutes):
- Divide the class into pairs. Assign each pair a common interview question to practice. Encourage students to take turns being the interviewer and interviewee. After each role-play, provide constructive feedback and switch roles.

Part 2: Formulating Thoughtful Questions (30 minutes)

1. Importance of Asking Questions (5 minutes):
- Discuss the significance of asking thoughtful questions during a college interview. Explain that it demonstrates genuine interest and curiosity about the college.

2. Examples of Thoughtful Questions (15 minutes):
- Provide examples of thoughtful questions that students can consider asking during their interviews. Discuss why these questions are effective in showcasing interest and engagement.

Examples of Thoughtful Questions:

- Can you tell me more about opportunities for undergraduate research in [specific field of study]?
- How would you describe the campus community and the relationship between students and professors?
- What support services are available for students who may need academic assistance?
- Can you share some notable accomplishments or recent initiatives by students at the college?
- How does the college support students in pursuing internships or experiential learning opportunities?

3. Student Question Formulation (10 minutes):
- Have each student write down three thoughtful questions they would like to ask during a college interview. Encourage them to consider specific aspects of the college that genuinely interest them.

4. Peer Feedback (5 minutes):
- Pairs of students can share their thoughtful questions with each other and provide feedback on clarity, relevance, and the potential impact on the interviewer.

Homework/Extended Activity (Optional):
- Assign students to conduct research on the colleges they are interested in and tailor their thoughtful questions to the specific institutions.

By practicing common interview questions and formulating thoughtful inquiries, students will build their confidence and approach college interviews with a prepared and engaged mindset. This exercise equips them with valuable skills for navigating this crucial aspect of the admissions process.

Discussion Questions

1. How did the monuments and landmarks in Washington, D.C., serve as a metaphor for Mr. Grant Money's sense of purpose? In what ways do physical spaces and symbols contribute to our understanding of personal and societal missions?

2. The meeting between Mr. Grant Money (MGM) and Cedric seemed almost serendipitous. How do chance encounters and unexpected connections play a role in shaping our life journeys, and how can mentorship during such encounters impact the trajectory of an individual's goals and aspirations?

3. The 7-point advice MGM provided to Cedric contains elements of both practicality and symbolism. How do the advice points not only guide Cedric in his college interview preparation but also symbolize broader themes of self-discovery, resilience, and the intergenerational transmission of knowledge?

4. MGM reflects on his ancestors and their contributions to the country while feeling a sense of purpose in empowering today's youth. How does the concept of legacy manifest in educational empowerment, and how can individuals draw inspiration from their heritage to guide and motivate the younger generations?

5. The National Museum of African American History and Culture becomes a pivotal setting for MGM's encounter with Cedric. How do museums and cultural institutions contribute to personal transformation and the shaping of one's values, especially in the context of education and societal progress?

 Big Idea "Virtual Mentorship Platform: "Legacy Guides"

Inspired by MGM's impactful encounter with Cedric, the idea is to create a virtual mentorship platform called "Legacy Guides." This platform connects experienced professionals, like MGM, with students seeking guidance for various aspects of their lives, be it education, career, or personal development. The platform could use a structured approach, incorporating video modules, live Q&A sessions, and personalized mentorship plans. It aims to bridge the gap between generations, enabling the transfer of knowledge and wisdom, much like the silent sentinels of history guiding the aspirations of the future.

🔍 Word Search

Embark on an enlightening word search puzzle journey inspired by the captivating tale of Mr. Grant Money, affectionately known as MGM, as he explores the historic wonders of Washington, D.C. This puzzle celebrates MGM's encounter with Cedric, a high school student with dreams of college, and the invaluable advice MGM imparts to guide Cedric on his path to success.

Join us in this word search adventure to discover the empowering words that echo the spirit of encouragement and aspiration found within the nation's capital.

Now, here are the 15 words for the word search puzzle based on the story:

M	E	N	C	O	U	R	A	G	E	M	E	N	T
L	L	A	N	D	M	A	R	K	S	E	M	N	S
A	I	G	P	E	R	M	E	A	M	G	O	M	W
C	A	P	I	T	O	L	E	S	H	U	N	O	N
R	E	S	I	L	I	E	N	C	E	A	E	C	A
A	S	E	H	U	M	U	H	H	P	R	Y	S	E
N	T	T	N	M	O	N	P	E	T	D	A	O	S
T	A	N	N	S	A	M	N	T	T	I	R	U	U
W	T	E	I	I	U	T	N	A	A	A	S	L	O
L	U	N	I	I	A	A	N	H	W	N	I	T	H
A	E	O	R	G	R	I	T	H	E	S	T	A	A
T	M	T	O	G	W	E	I	V	R	E	T	N	I
U	N	N	E	E	P	T	S	W	A	C	S	T	C
M	O	N	U	M	E	N	T	D	U	P	O	M	H

MONUMENT
GUARDIANS
WHITE
PENTAGON
LANDMARKS
RESILIENCE
SOUL
ENCOURAGEMENT
INTERVIEW
STATUE
TRIUMPH
GRANT
HOUSE
MONEY
CAPITOL

MR. GRANT MONEY

"In the delicate dance of serendipity, two worlds converged within the walls of history. A butterfly on a shoulder, a meeting orchestrated by fate. Cedric, with dreams soaring higher than the museum's spire, found in MGM not just advice but a torchbearer lighting the way for dreams yet to be realized. In the tapestry of shared stories, a thread of guidance was woven, connecting past and future."

SUCCESS STORIES

"Guided by Destiny: Jellianne's Triumph through Mentorship, Self-Reflection, and College Success"

In the bustling city of Baltimore, Maryland, Jellianne, a determined high school student, found herself at a crossroads as she prepared to embark on her college journey. She had always dreamt of attending a prestigious university, but the challenges of the college application process loomed large. The prospect of college interviews, in particular, left her feeling anxious and uncertain.

Jellianne's encounter with destiny began during a visit to the National Museum of African American History and Culture in Washington, D.C. It was there that her path converged with that of Mr. Grant Money, or MGM, a mentor with a wealth of experience. In their serendipitous meeting, Jellianne shared her aspirations and fears, especially regarding the impending college interviews.

MGM, ever the compassionate guide, offered Jellianne a treasure trove of advice. His 7-point plan for college interviews became her roadmap to success. Jellianne embraced self-reflection, delved into meticulous research about her chosen colleges, practiced her responses diligently, and prepared thoughtful questions for her interviewers. With a renewed sense of purpose, she felt better equipped to tackle the interview process.

As Jellianne embarked on her college interviews, she carried MGM's wisdom with her. Her interviews were marked by confidence, poise, and a genuine enthusiasm for her chosen field of study. She impressed her interviewers not only with her academic achievements but also with her resilience, growth, and passion for learning.

Months later, the college acceptance letters arrived, and Jellianne's heart swelled with pride. She had been admitted to her dream university, a testament to her unwavering determination and the transformative mentorship she had received from MGM. Her success story was a beacon of hope and inspiration for aspiring students in her community.

Jellianne's journey continued beyond her college acceptance. She thrived academically and personally, determined to make the most of her college experience. As she reflected on her path, she knew that her encounter with MGM and the wisdom he shared had been a turning point in her life. Jellianne had not only fulfilled her dreams but also gained the confidence to pursue her passions and embrace her heritage.

With a heart full of gratitude, Jellianne knew that her story would inspire generations to come, highlighting the power of mentorship, self-reflection, and determination in achieving one's aspirations. She looked forward to the exciting adventures that awaited her in college, carrying with her the legacy of those who had paved the way, just as MGM had done for her.

Beyond the Leather: Mr. Grant Money's Guide to College Elegance

Step Into the World of High-End Boutiques and Academia as Mr. Grant Money Shares His Adventures"

Mr. Grant Money found himself in the vibrant city of Los Angeles for the weekend, and one thing he couldn't resist was indulging in a visit to one of his favorite men's boutique shoe stores on the illustrious Rodeo Drive. The finely manicured storefronts and designer boutiques exuded luxury, but the promise of finding the perfect pair of shoes drew him in.

As he strolled through the carefully curated selection of fine Italian shoes, his discerning eyes spotted a pair that seemed to beckon him. Crafted with precision and elegance, these shoes were a work of art. Mr. Grant Money envisioned himself donning them for a special gala he was set to attend the next day.

With excitement in his eyes, he approached the store clerk and requested the shoes in his size. However, to his dismay, as clerk brought them over, Mr. Grant Money realized that they were an uncomfortably tight fit. He winced as he tried to wiggle his toes into the exquisite leather, and the discomfort was palpable. Requesting a larger size, he was met with the disappointing news that the shoe was no longer in production and no larger sizes were available.

The decision was clear: forcing himself into those beautiful but painfully tight shoes would result in a miserable night. Mr. Grant Money gracefully passed on the pair, acknowledging that true elegance is not just in appearance but in comfort too. Undeterred, he decided to explore another high-end boutique just a few blocks away.

At the next store, he discovered a pair of shoes that looked great and fit him perfectly. They exceeded his expectations and, as fate would have it, turned out to be one of his favorite pairs. The lesson was clear – sometimes, what seems like a setback is merely guiding us toward a better fit.

Later, seated at a nearby restaurant, Mr. Grant Money took out his Golden Journal and jotted down five essential considerations for students to ensure the right college fit:

1. Academic Alignment
- Ensure that the college offers the academic programs and majors that align with your interests and career goals. The right fit extends beyond appearances.

2. Campus Culture
- Consider the campus culture and atmosphere. Are you comfortable with the size of the student body, the social scene, and the overall vibe of the campus?

3. Extracurricular Opportunities
- Evaluate the availability of extracurricular activities and clubs that resonate with your passions. A well-rounded college experience goes beyond the classroom.

4. Support Services
- Investigate the support services available, such as academic advising, counseling, and career guidance. A supportive environment can significantly impact your success.

5. Financial Fit
- Assess the financial aspects, including tuition, fees, and available financial aid. Finding a balance that aligns with your budget and long-term financial goals is crucial.

In the end, Mr. Grant Money stressed the importance of not forcing a fit when a perfect match is waiting. Much like finding the right pair of shoes, discovering the ideal college involves patience, consideration, and a willingness to explore beyond initial setbacks. The lesson was clear – in the vast landscape of colleges, there's a perfect fit for each student if they can only let go of what might be holding them back at the moment.

Exercise: "Finding Your College Fit"

Objective: This exercise is designed to guide students in exploring and evaluating factors that contribute to finding the right college fit. By engaging in self-reflection and research, students will identify key considerations for their college decision-making process.

Materials Needed:
1. Notebooks or paper
2. Writing implements
3. Access to the internet for research (optional)

Steps:

1. Introduction (10 minutes):
- Begin the exercise by discussing the importance of finding the right college fit. Emphasize that the college experience extends beyond academics and involves various factors that contribute to a student's overall satisfaction and success.

2. Self-Reflection (15 minutes):
- Ask students to take some time for self-reflection. Have them consider their academic interests, personal preferences, and goals for the college experience. Encourage them to jot down their thoughts on the following questions:

- What academic programs or majors are you interested in?
- What size of campus and student body do you envision yourself thriving in?
- What type of campus culture and social scene aligns with your preferences?
- Are there specific extracurricular activities or clubs you want to engage in?
- What support services, such as academic advising or counseling, do you think would be beneficial for your success?

3. Researching Potential Colleges (30 minutes):
- Instruct students to research colleges that align with their reflections from Step 2. They can use college websites, reviews, and other resources to gather information on academic programs, campus culture, extracurricular opportunities, and support services. Encourage them to create a list of colleges that seem like potential fits.

4. Evaluating Financial Considerations (15 minutes):

- Discuss the importance of financial considerations in the college decision-making process. Students should assess the cost of tuition, fees, and available financial aid options. Provide guidance on understanding the financial fit of each college.

5. Developing a Personal Criteria Checklist (20 minutes):

- Have students create a personal criteria checklist based on their reflections and research. This checklist should include factors like academic alignment, campus culture, extracurricular opportunities, support services, and financial considerations. Encourage them to prioritize these factors based on personal importance.

6. Reflection and Sharing (15 minutes):

- After completing the checklist, ask students to reflect on the process. What did they discover about their preferences and priorities? Students can share their reflections with a partner or the class, fostering discussion and insights.

7. Peer Feedback (15 minutes):

- Pair students up to review each other's personal criteria checklists. Encourage constructive feedback and suggestions. This collaborative process can help students refine their considerations and gain perspectives from their peers.

Homework/Extended Activity (Optional):

- Assign students to further research and narrow down their list of potential colleges based on their personal criteria. This can include reaching out to college admissions offices for additional information.

By engaging in this exercise, students gain valuable insights into their preferences and priorities, making the college decision-making process more informed and tailored to their needs.

"Just as I passed on those beautifully crafted shoes that pinched my toes, remember, students, a college that doesn't fit comfortably academically, socially, and financially may look appealing but will bring you nothing but discomfort in the long run. Invest wisely in your education, and the right fit will carry you elegantly through life's journey."

- Mr. Grant Money

Discussion Questions

1. Reflecting on Mr. Grant Money's experience with the uncomfortable but visually appealing shoes, how can this metaphor be applied to the college selection process? Are there instances where students might be tempted by prestigious or visually appealing colleges but risk sacrificing their comfort and fit academically or socially?

2. In Mr. Grant Money's journey, he encountered setbacks but eventually found a better fit. How can students navigate setbacks during their college search, and what advice would you give to someone who might be facing challenges in finding the right academic or cultural fit?

3. Considering the five essential considerations Mr. Grant Money outlined in his Golden Journal for college selection, which one do you think is often overlooked or underestimated by students? How might neglecting any of these factors impact a student's overall college experience?

4. Mr. Grant Money emphasizes the importance of not forcing a fit when searching for the perfect pair of shoes or the ideal college. Can you share personal experiences or examples of individuals who, by being patient and open-minded, discovered a college that turned out to be a perfect fit despite initial setbacks or uncertainties?

5. Drawing parallels between the shoe shopping experience and the college selection process, how can prospective students strike a balance between aspirations and realistic expectations? What advice would you offer to someone who has set their sights on a particular college but may need to reconsider due to factors like academic alignment, campus culture, or financial fit?

 Big Idea "Virtual College Tours with a Personal Touch"

Create a platform that offers virtual college tours enriched with personal experiences and insights from current students. This platform could go beyond the standard virtual tours by incorporating real stories about academic alignment, campus culture, extracurricular opportunities, support services, and financial fit. Students could virtually connect with current students who share similar interests or career goals, providing a more authentic and personalized perspective. This initiative aims to bridge the gap between the glossy brochures and the reality of college life, helping prospective students make more informed decisions about their college fit.

🔍 Word Search

Welcome to the "Mr. Grant Money Wordsearch Puzzle," inspired by the fashionable adventures of Mr. Grant Money in the vibrant city of Los Angeles. As he embarked on a quest for the perfect pair of shoes, his journey led him to valuable lessons about the importance of finding the right fit whether it be in footwear or higher education.

Now, dive into the puzzle and search for the words related to Mr. Grant Money's story and the essential considerations for finding the perfect college fit

Now, here are the 14 words for the word search puzzle based on the story:

S	T	R	O	F	M	O	C	S	N	E	T	A	C
L	S	E	L	E	G	A	N	C	E	O	T	O	O
O	A	E	O	Q	A	L	S	E	G	D	C	S	T
M	E	I	A	S	B	E	O	A	R	N	O	O	O
E	I	L	R	E	O	S	S	C	S	E	S	L	A
C	A	A	P	T	U	S	D	E	D	L	C	E	J
O	C	I	S	B	T	O	U	O	D	E	E	R	T
O	A	C	D	A	I	N	R	P	A	T	C	A	L
L	D	N	E	C	Q	S	R	A	P	S	O	R	A
O	E	A	S	K	U	O	A	P	R	O	E	S	N
N	M	N	H	C	E	A	L	A	G	F	R	R	R
M	I	I	O	S	R	O	J	A	M	R	P	T	U
A	C	F	E	X	P	L	O	R	E	A	D	E	O
G	A	A	S	L	O	O	U	E	T	T	S	O	J

RODEO
GALA
LESSONS
ELEGANCE
JOURNAL
ACADEMIC
SETBACK
SUPPORT
BOUTIQUE
SHOES
COMFORT
MAJORS
EXPLORE
FINANCIAL

"Life, much like Mr. Grant Money's quest for the perfect pair of shoes, teaches us that sometimes what seems like a setback is just a redirection towards a better fit. In choosing a college, don't force yourself into an ill-suited institution; instead, embrace the journey of exploration. The right academic, social, and financial fit awaits those who have the patience to seek it beyond initial setbacks."

SUCCESS STORIES

"Finding the Perfect Fit: Maureen's Journey from Crossroads to Academic Home"

Maureen, a high school senior with lofty dreams, found herself at a pivotal crossroads—choosing the right college to shape her future. Like Mr. Grant Money's quest for the perfect pair of shoes on Rodeo Drive, Maureen sought not just any college but the one that would align with her aspirations and values. As the pressure of college applications loomed, she encountered moments of doubt and uncertainty, wondering if she would ever discover the institution that truly resonated with her.

Inspired by the parallel between her journey and Mr. Grant Money's quest, Maureen resolved to find the ideal college fit. She diligently researched her options, meticulously evaluating factors such as academic alignment, campus culture, extracurricular opportunities, support services, and financial fit. Through this thorough exploration, she aimed to discover the institution that would nurture her growth and passion.

In due course, Maureen received acceptance letters from various colleges, but one stood out as a perfect match. This college offered the academic program she was deeply passionate about, embraced a vibrant campus culture, and provided an array of extracurricular opportunities. The comprehensive support services and a well-suited financial aid package solidified her decision. It was a comfortable fit, much like Mr. Grant Money's favorite pair of shoes, and Maureen knew she had found her academic home.

In the ensuing years, Maureen thrived at her chosen college, excelling academically, pursuing her passions, and making a meaningful impact through extracurricular engagement. Her story exemplified the power of prioritizing the right fit in life's pivotal decisions. As Maureen looked ahead to a bright future, she cherished the wisdom she had gained from an unexpected source—the tale of a pair of shoes on Rodeo Drive.

Coding Dreams and Blogging Brilliance: The Unseen Path to Silicon Valley Success

Join Mr. Grant Money on a Tech Odyssey as Two High School Wonders Craft Their Extracurricular Narratives for the Hallowed Halls of Stanford

In the heart of Silicon Valley, where innovation thrived and dreams were crafted in lines of code, Mr. Grant Money found himself immersed in a story of ambition, passion, and extracurricular excellence.

Camille and Emily, two high school students with a shared fascination for technology, were determined to make their mark in the tech world. Their eyes were set on the illustrious Stanford University, nestled in the heart of the valley, and they knew that their college applications needed to shine with extracurricular excellence.

One sunny afternoon, Mr. Grant Money met Camille and Emily at a bustling tech expo in Silicon Valley. The air was charged with the excitement of groundbreaking inventions and entrepreneurial spirit. The two students, wide-eyed and eager, approached Mr. Grant Money seeking guidance on how to stand out in the competitive college application process.

Seated at a futuristic exhibit showcasing the latest in artificial intelligence, Mr. Grant Money listened intently to Camille and Emily's aspirations. Both were deeply involved in coding clubs, hackathons, and collaborative projects, but they felt the pressure to elevate their extracurricular profiles.

With his trademark enthusiasm, Mr. Grant Money shared insights that would soon set the stage for their extracurricular excellence journey.

Camille's Story:

Camille, a brilliant coder with a passion for developing apps that could make a difference, was struggling to convey her impact in a way that stood out. Mr. Grant Money encouraged her to create a portfolio showcasing her projects, complete with explanations of the problems she aimed to solve and the innovative solutions she devised. He stressed the importance of not just listing activities but telling a compelling story of her journey in technology.

Inspired, Camille spent the next few weeks crafting a visually stunning portfolio. She highlighted her involvement in coding competitions, open-source contributions, and the app she developed to help local businesses during the pandemic. Her portfolio not only showcased technical prowess but also the real-world impact of her work.

Emily's Story:

Emily, an aspiring tech entrepreneur, was deeply involved in organizing hackathons and mentoring younger students. However, she struggled to convey the leadership and teamwork skills she gained from these experiences. Mr. Grant Money suggested that Emily create a blog where she could share her insights, experiences, and the lessons learned from organizing hackathons.

Following this advice, Emily launched a blog titled "TechTrailblazer." She documented the challenges of event planning, highlighted the success stories of participants, and shared her vision for fostering a collaborative tech community. The blog not only demonstrated her leadership skills but also showcased her ability to articulate her journey in a way that resonated with readers.

As college application season unfolded, Camille and Emily submitted their applications to Stanford, each armed with a unique representation of their extracurricular excellence.

Months later, Mr. Grant Money received a heartwarming update. Camille and Emily had not only been accepted into Stanford University but had also caught the attention of tech industry leaders impressed by their portfolios and blog. Their stories became an inspiration for future students in Silicon Valley, proving that extracurricular excellence, when crafted with passion and purpose, could open doors to limitless possibilities.

In his Golden Journal, Mr. Grant Money noted the transformative power of extracurricular storytelling and left with a quote echoing in his mind: "In the world of innovation, the stories we tell about our journey are as important as the code we write." With a sense of fulfillment, he continued on his journey, leaving behind two young tech trailblazers ready to shape the future of Silicon Valley.

"In the heart of Silicon Valley, where dreams are coded into reality, remember this: your extracurricular journey is the canvas, and your story is the masterpiece. Craft it with passion, narrate it with purpose, and watch as the doors of possibility swing wide open."

- Mr. Grant Money

Exercise: "Crafting Your Extracurricular Story"

Objective: This exercise aims to guide students in articulating their extracurricular experiences in a compelling way. By creating a portfolio or blog entry, students will learn how to effectively convey the impact of their activities and stand out in the college application process.

Materials Needed:
1. Notebooks or paper
2. Access to a computer or paper and markers for those creating physical portfolios

Steps:

1. Introduction (10 minutes):
- Begin by discussing the significance of presenting extracurricular activities in a compelling way during the college application process. Emphasize the importance of showcasing not just the activities themselves but the impact and lessons learned.

2. Self-Reflection (15 minutes):
- Ask students to reflect on their extracurricular activities. What projects or experiences have been particularly meaningful to them? What skills have they gained, and how have they made a positive impact? Encourage them to jot down key points.

3. Choose a Format (10 minutes):
- Present students with the option to create either a digital portfolio or a blog entry. If they choose a digital portfolio, suggest platforms like Adobe Portfolio or Google Sites. If they prefer a blog, platforms like Medium or WordPress can be recommended. Those opting for a physical portfolio can use paper, markers, and any creative materials available.

"To those navigating the tech realms of ambition, never forget that your impact transcends lines of code. Your journey is a symphony of innovation, and each extracurricular note is a key to unlock futures yet to be imagined. Play your story with fervor, and the world will listen."

- Mr. Grant Money

4. Create Content (40 minutes):

– Guide students through the process of creating content for their chosen format. Each entry should include the following elements:

- Introduction: A brief overview of the student's interests and the purpose of the portfolio or blog.
- Projects/Activities: Detailed descriptions of specific projects or activities, emphasizing the skills developed and the impact on others or the community.
- Challenges and Growth: Reflection on challenges faced during these activities and the personal or professional growth achieved.
- Lessons Learned: Insights gained from extracurricular experiences and how they contribute to the student's overall story.
- Visuals: Include visuals such as photos, screenshots, or any relevant media to enhance the storytelling.

5. Peer Feedback (15 minutes):

– Encourage students to share their portfolios or blog drafts with a peer for constructive feedback. Emphasize the importance of clarity, impact, and storytelling. Peers can provide suggestions on how to enhance the narrative.

6. Revisions and Finalization (20 minutes):

– Based on peer feedback, students should revise and finalize their portfolios or blog entries. Remind them to pay attention to the overall presentation, ensuring that it reflects their unique journey and showcases their extracurricular excellence effectively.

7. Reflection (10 minutes):

– Conclude the exercise with a reflection session. Students can share what they learned about their own experiences through the process of creating their portfolios or blog entries. Discuss the importance of storytelling in making extracurricular activities stand out.

This exercise not only enhances students' ability to communicate their extracurricular achievements but also provides them with valuable skills in self-reflection and digital storytelling, which are beneficial beyond the college application process.

Discussion Questions

1. How did Mr. Grant Money's advice about creating a compelling narrative impact Camille and Emily's approach to showcasing their extracurricular activities, and what role do storytelling and personal narratives play in the college application process?

2. In the competitive landscape of Silicon Valley and the tech industry, how did Camille and Emily leverage their extracurricular experiences to not only stand out in their college applications but also capture the attention of tech industry leaders? What does this say about the value of extracurricular excellence in shaping future career opportunities?

3. The story highlights the importance of not just participating in extracurricular activities but also strategically representing those experiences. How do you think Camille's visually stunning portfolio and Emily's "TechTrailblazer" blog contributed to their success, and what can other students learn from their approaches in presenting their extracurricular journeys?

4. Mr. Grant Money emphasized the transformative power of extracurricular storytelling. In your opinion, how might this concept apply beyond college applications? Can the art of storytelling be influential in other aspects of personal and professional development, especially in the realm of innovation and entrepreneurship?

5. Camille and Emily each faced specific challenges in conveying the impact of their activities. How did their distinct approaches—Camille with a visually stunning portfolio and Emily with a blog—reflect their individual strengths and aspirations? What does this reveal about tailoring one's presentation of extracurricular excellence to align with personal goals and interests?

 Big Idea "Innovation Impact Showcase"

Organize an annual event or competition where students can present their tech projects along with the stories behind them. This could be a physical expo or a virtual event, bringing together students, mentors, and industry professionals. The emphasis would be on the narrative – students would not only showcase their technical skills but also explain the problems they aimed to solve and the journey of creating solutions. Industry leaders could judge the projects based on both technical merit and the ability to communicate the impact of their work. This showcase not only becomes a platform for recognition but also an opportunity for students to refine their storytelling skills in a competitive yet supportive environment.

🔍 Word Search

Embark on an exciting word search adventure inspired by the captivating story of Camille and Emily, two high school students navigating the competitive landscape of Silicon Valley with dreams of making a mark in the tech world. Mr. Grant Money, a guiding force in their journey, shared valuable insights that propelled them toward extracurricular excellence.

As you search for the hidden words in this puzzle, discover key elements from their stories and the transformative power of crafting a compelling narrative.

Now, here are the 14 words for the word search puzzle based on the story:

H	R	L	E	T	E	C	H	N	O	L	O	G	Y
C	E	C	N	I	N	N	O	V	A	T	I	O	N
O	Z	L	T	P	O	R	T	F	O	L	I	O	T
L	A	A	R	T	L	N	O	I	S	S	A	P	S
L	L	U	E	R	E	V	A	L	L	E	Y	Y	N
A	B	E	P	R	A	A	N	I	L	O	E	K	O
B	L	O	R	I	D	E	A	E	S	N	C	S	H
O	I	C	E	N	E	R	O	R	R	L	H	R	T
R	A	O	N	I	R	R	R	U	L	A	R	D	A
A	R	D	E	Y	S	O	O	L	L	S	E	B	K
T	T	I	U	P	H	J	D	E	P	X	V	E	C
I	A	N	R	I	I	H	I	E	P	R	T	G	A
V	D	G	R	R	P	T	E	O	R	R	R	O	H
E	E	D	R	O	F	N	A	T	S	R	T	O	N

ENTREPRENEUR
JOURNEY
PORTFOLIO
STANFORD
VALLEY
HACKATHONS
COLLABORATIVE
INNOVATION
EXPO
CODING
TRAILBLAZER
LEADERSHIP
PASSION
TECHNOLOGY

"In the dance of ambition and innovation, the steps you take are as vital as the dreams you chase. Extracurricular excellence is not merely a list; it's a narrative, a journey penned with passion and purpose. In the grand ballroom of life, let your story be the waltz that captivates hearts and opens doors."

SUCCESS STORIES

"Breaking the Mold: Sophia Chen's Journey from After-School Robotics to Silicon Valley Powerhouse"

Sophia Chen wasn't your typical Silicon Valley success story. She wasn't a prodigy coder at 10 or the founder of a startup before college. In fact, her passion didn't even begin with technology. It started in the art studio of her high school, where she led a small group of classmates in designing intricate, futuristic sculptures.

But something clicked when Sophia joined the after-school robotics club during her junior year. Initially, she was drawn to the design aspect —shaping the robot's aesthetic. Yet as the team faced challenges in functionality, she immersed herself in learning the engineering and coding aspects. By senior year, Sophia wasn't just designing robots; she was programming them, integrating AI algorithms that helped her team win regional championships.

It was her multidisciplinary approach that stood out. At Stanford, where she double-majored in Mechanical Engineering and Studio Arts, Sophia founded SymbioTech, a nonprofit that brought coding workshops to underserved schools but with a twist—they combined tech lessons with creative arts. She believed the next generation of innovators would need to think beyond lines of code and embrace creativity as their edge.

Today, Sophia is the CEO of Visionary Robotics, a Silicon Valley unicorn that blends AI, robotics, and artistic design into products that revolutionize healthcare, education, and environmental sustainability. She's also an advocate for "extracurricular innovation," believing her success wasn't just about mastering tech but about combining tech with the passions that make us human.

"Don't just build something that works," Sophia often says. "Build something that inspires."

AFTERWARD

As you reach the final pages of The Amazing Adventures of Mr. Grant Money, Volume 2, I hope you've been both entertained and enlightened by the captivating stories of our enigmatic protagonist, Mr. Grant Money. Through his remarkable adventures, you've explored the world of grants and philanthropy in an entirely new light.

These stories are not just tales of daring exploits and awe-inspiring achievements. They are also valuable lessons in grant acquisition, each with its unique insights and wisdom. However, the true magic happens when you put these lessons into practice. Remember, knowledge without action is like a locked treasure chest; it holds immense potential, but only when you open it does its true value become apparent.

It's important to recognize that in the world of grant acquisition, we all start at ground zero. What separates the triumphant from the rest is the determination to progress beyond that initial point. After reading these stories, take a moment to reflect on the lessons they impart and how you can apply them to your own journey in grant acquisition.

And there's no need to stop here! Mr. Grant Money's adventures continue with even more fascinating tales in Volumes 3 through 5. As you embark on these new journeys, embrace the valuable insights they offer. Keep in mind that knowledge, like a never-ending treasure trove, continues to expand. By continuing to learn and adapt, you too can achieve remarkable results in the world of grants and philanthropy.

If you're looking for further guidance and resources, consider visiting GrantCentralUSA.com and GrantAcquisition.com. These platforms offer a wealth of tools, courses, and expert advice to enhance your grant acquisition skills.

Remember, the key to success in grant acquisition is not just in learning but in applying what you've learned. As Mr. Grant Money has demonstrated, each adventure is an opportunity for growth, and your journey is no different. The power to make a difference in your community and beyond is within your grasp.

So, gear up for the next volumes of Mr. Grant Money's incredible adventures, and keep striving to transform your grant acquisition endeavors into triumphant tales of your own. Your journey is just beginning, and there's no limit to what you can achieve. The world of grants and philanthropy is waiting for your story to unfold, and the possibilities are limitless.

ABOUT THE AUTHOR

Rodney Walker is a man on a mission. He's dedicated his life to helping others secure funding for their projects and dreams. As the President of Grant Central USA, a grant development training firm internationally known for helping organizations land six-figure and seven-figure grants and shave months off the time it takes to get funded, Rodney has helped clients raise over half a billion dollars in grants!

He's also an author of numerous books, online courses and the founder of two popular grant writing conferences: The Education Grants Conference and First Responders Grants Conference. Grant Central USA has also partnered with several universities, including Regis University, Hawaii University, Oklahoma University, National University, Cal Poly University, and Florida Atlantic University.

Rodney is even the host of four podcasts: Get Funded with Rodney, Grant Writing Today, Grant Business Show, and Schools Winning Grants. He oversees Grant Success Advisors, an elite network of approved licensees who deliver today's leading training in grant development systems.

He has an extensive network of high-level contacts, including his Grant Writers Association group on Linkedin with over 15,000+ members.

Considered a national authority in the grant industry, Grant Central USA's clients have included, The Magic Johnson Foundation, the George W. Bush Foundation, Ben Guillory and Danny Glover of the Robey Theatre Company, Hawaii State Teachers Association, United Way, Habitat for Humanity, and numerous school districts and city governments.

Rodney has produced over 730 videos on grant development on his popular YouTube channel and has taught over 240,000 people how to improve their grant writing efforts. "We have been helping our clients successfully get funded and launch new careers in grant writing since 2006 across the U.S. and worldwide, giving them both the competence and the confidence to win the grants at a high level."

He says his primary specialty is "Getting our clients funded with six-figure and seven-figure grants while helping grant professionals get paid what they are worth!"

In addition to his leadership experience at Grant Central USA, he has years of experience in Business and Professional Development in various sectors. He has been a sought-after expert in grant professional development, coaching, and the law of success.

As a media personality, he has interviewed numerous celebrities, including Snoop Dogg, Heisman Trophy Winners: Reggie Bush, Charles Woodson, Professional Boxer Laila Ali, America's Next Top Model Season 19 Winner: Laura James, NBA Champions: Draymond Green, Matt Barnes, National College Football Champions: Coach Mack Brown, and Vince Young, and countless others.

It's safe to say that Rodney knows his stuff regarding grants and working with champions!

MGM Music to Get You Going 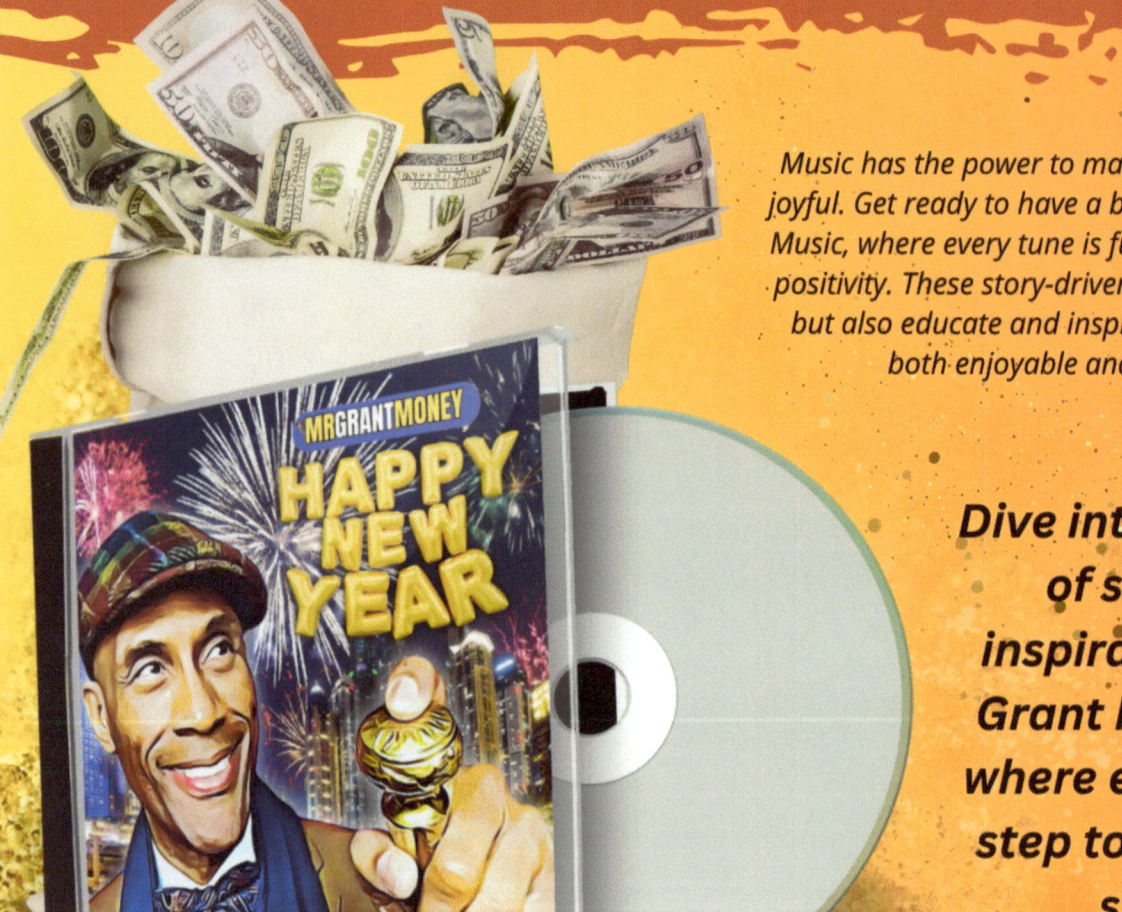 and 🎶 Keep You Soaring!

Music has the power to make life and learning more joyful. Get ready to have a blast with Mr. Grant Money Music, where every tune is fun, upbeat, and filled with positivity. These story-driven songs not only entertain but also educate and inspire, making your journey both enjoyable and enriching. 🎶

Dive into a symphony of stories and inspiration with Mr. Grant Money Music, where every note is a step toward greater success.

You can enjoy Mr. Grant Money Music on most major streaming platforms, including Spotify, Apple Music, and Amazon Music, bringing inspiration and positivity right to your favorite device. 🎧

Diverse Musical Flavors to Satisfy Every Listening Craving

Topical and Seasonal Themes

Enjoy our themed musical sessions that align with the seasons and current events, offering fresh perspectives and innovative ideas from today's Top Master Grant Acquisition Specialist, Mr. Grant Money!

Experience Our Other Dynamic Series with Mr. Grant Money!

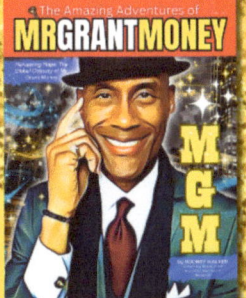

Harvesting Hope: The Global Odyssey of Mr. Grant Money

Vol. 1

ISBN 978-0-9659275-0-5

The Artful Navigator: Mr. Grant Money's Chronicles

Vol. 2

ISBN 978-0-9659275-2-9

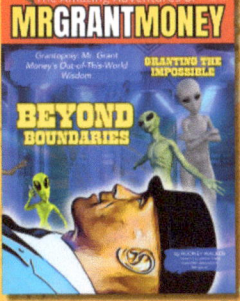

Grantopoly: Mr. Grant Money's Out-of-This-World Wisdom

Vol. 3

ISBN 978-0-9659275-3-6

Grant Odyssey: Mr. Grant Money's Time-Traveling Feats

Vol. 4

ISBN 978-0-9659275-4-3

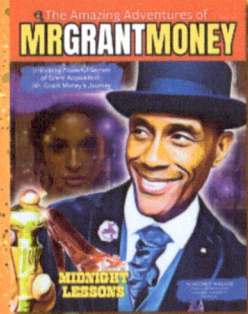

Unlocking Powerful Secrets of Grant Acquisition

Vol. 5

ISBN 978-0-9659275-5-0

The Entrepreneurial Classroom: Teens Redefining Success

Vol. 1

ISBN 979-8-89725-005-9

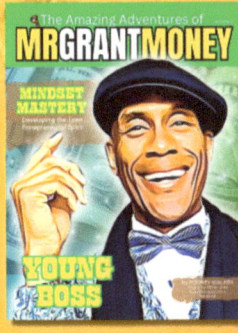

Mindset Mastery: Developing The Teen Entrepreneurial Spirit

Vol. 2

ISBN 979-8-89725-006-6

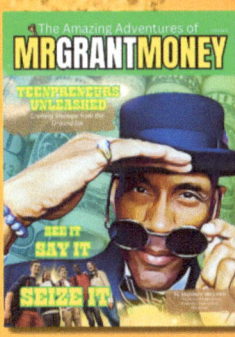

Teenpreneurs Unleashed: Crafting Startups From The Ground Up

Vol. 3

ISBN 979-8-89725-007-3

Business Battlefront: Teens Conquering Challenges In Startups

Vol. 4

ISBN 979-8-89725-008-0

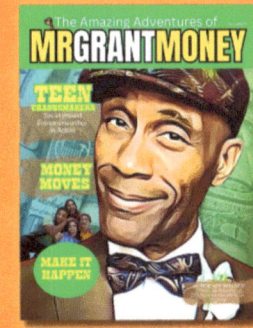

Teen Changemakers: Social Impact Entrepreneurship in Action

Vol. 5

ISBN 979-8-89725-009-7

Pocket Power: A Guide to Practical Budgeting for Teens

Vol. 1

ISBN 979-8-89725-010-3

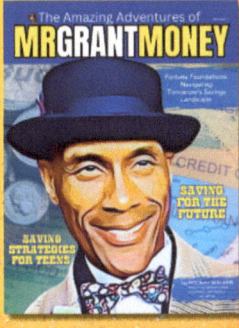

Fortune Foundations: Navigating Tomorrow's Savings Landscape

Vol. 2

ISBN 979-8-89725-011-0

Profit Pioneers: Young Entrepreneurs Unleashed

Vol. 3

ISBN 979-8-89725-012-7

Scholarly Cents: A College Finance Expedition

Vol. 4

ISBN 979-8-89725-013-4

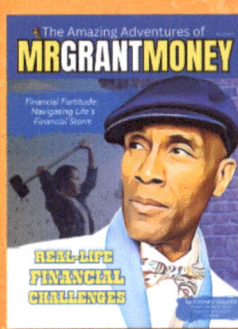

Financial Fortitude: Navigating Life's Financial Storm

Vol. 5

ISBN 979-8-89725-014-1

Win More Scholarship In Less Time with These...

"Thank you so much for your help. Probably not a day has gone by that I didn't use something."
— Evelyn Barker, Director of Grants and Special Project at University of Texas

Elevate your scholarship efforts into success with my proven strategies that have raised millions.

Scholarship Success Secret is not just a guide; it's a storytelling journey like no other. Across five compelling books, Mr. Grant Money—takes you into the lives of students, parents, and educators.

Through these vivid, relatable tales, you'll uncover the insider secrets, proven strategies, and practical steps to secure the scholarships and education grants you need for college and beyond.

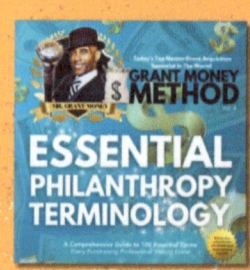
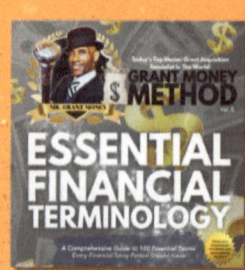

Boost your confidence in grant writing, fundraising, and finance! Elevate your communication skills with the **Fundraising Fundamentals Vocabulary Builder Series** – *100 essential terms in each series.* Invest in knowledge, empower your success!

Enjoy More Amazing Adventures with Mr. Grant Money!

Scholarship Odyssey:
Mr. Grant Money's Roadmap

Vol. 1

ISBN 979-8-89725-000-4

Journey To Acceptance:
Navigating College Applications

Vol. 2

ISBN 979-8-89725-001-1

Passion Into Practice:
Specialized Scholarship

Vol. 3

ISBN 979-8-89725-002-8

Passport To Success:
Navigating Global Scholarships

Vol. 4

ISBN 979-8-89725-003-5

Empowering Futures:
Scholarships With Lasting Impact

Vol. 5

ISBN 979-8-89725-004-2

Gain Exclusive Access To Companion Resources & Bonus Materials at MrGrantMoney.com and GrantCentralUsa.com

LICENSED

Bring the transformative Adventures and lessons of Mr. Grant Money to your educational institution or organization by **acquiring your license today**. Enjoy exclusive access to a wealth of online resources, such as special reports, worksheets, videos, audio training, discounts, and more, elevating the entire experience to the next level!

Envision and affirm your grant success in the same proactive spirit as Mr. Grant Money. **Experience the power of these daily affirmations** to inspire and motivate your journey toward success!